Angel City Review
A Ten Year Retrospective of LA Poetry
Edited By Zachary C Jensen

Angel City Review is a volunteer run literary journal born in Los Angeles CA in 2014. The focus is primarily on writings from Los Angeles that highlight the diverse voices and styles contemporary poetry and prose has to offer. From its inception, it has always been considered a community service and based project. This is a labor of love and takes no profit from the work it produces.

Publication Data:

Name: Zachary C Jensen (Editor)
Title: Angel City Review
Subtitle: A Ten Year Retrospective of LA Poetry
Description: First Edition. | Los Angeles, CA : Angel City Review, [2025]
Identifiers: ISBN 979-8-218-62367-8
Subjects: Poetry / American / General

Supported by funding from Accelerate Resilience L.A., a sponsored project of Rockefeller Philanthropy Advisors

Thank you to all the editors who have volunteered their time, energy, and passion over the years, the journal could not have existed without you. This is especially true for John Venegas.

A special thank you to Norma for all your support and care.

Table of Contents:

Introduction

Los Angeles is a unique city, a sprawling metropolis that almost demands that you drive through its palm tree-lined streets. It drew over four hundred thousand transplants to the city in 2024 alone; people with the singular notion of the place as the home of fame, fortune, and celebrity found through music, film, streaming, or art. This notion is one that has become popularized in television and film. It is then further reinforced when many transplants choose to insulate themselves in pockets of gentrification, where the only people they meet are other transplants because they have pushed out the communities that were already there. But this very narrow view leaves out all the other vibrant layers of culture, history, and stories that rest in our soil. There is an incredible diversity of people and experiences that can be found in every neighborhood, people whose contributions to this city are the true foundations of what it is built on. Not what you find on TV.

This single-story fallacy is something we have striven to avoid in our work at Angel City Review. Since our inception in 2014, we have always understood that the city is comprised of multiple communities, and we have done our best to shine light on as many as we could. Over the years, we have had the honor of publishing some amazing poets from Los Angeles as well as beyond, writers whose unique view of the world, when expressed in their poetry, were able to share something universal. People who documented histories, told stories, fought injustices, celebrated love, grieved loss, and shared space for more than just people who looked like them. Even when someone was writing about their specific cultural experiences, it gave others the opportunity to see the whole of them, but also let readers know that their experience held value.

While we have published writers from across the United States as well as the world, our hearts have always been firmly planted in Los Angeles. For this anthology, we chose to highlight some of the best poetry we have published these past ten years by poets who either live in or are connected to the city we call home. It can also function as a focused survey of contemporary Los Angeles poetry, not just in name, but in style and form as well. Some of the names you may very well recognize, while others may be entirely new to you. Many of the writers in these pages had only a small handful of journal publications when we published them and now have multiple books to their name. There are even a few whose poetry wowed us at the time but then chose to go in other directions with their lives. We by no means claim that these are the only poets that matter in Los Angeles. There are so many writers we admire that we have never had the chance to publish. But these forty-four names are more than worth reading.

In keeping with the theme of having art in every issue of the journal, we partnered with the Charlie James Gallery in Los Angeles to feature some LA based artists that are doing exciting work today. Their work speaks to the principles and ideas that we hold. Their work is often an examination and celebration of culture, of diversity, of experiences that deserve shining light on. They are also very distinctly LA in their style and ethos. When looking at their work, it just feels like the city.

Lastly, when thinking about how to organize the collection, we settled on a chronological approach. Writers who were in our first issue start us off and we close with those who were in issue thirteen. A few writers were in our issues more than once, and in that case, all their poems were placed together in order of their first appearance. We hope that by reading this book, you get a glimpse of the multitude of stories that Los Angeles has to offer.

-       Zachary C Jensen

Danie Cansino - Fowler Street

Lost in Ravenna

By Dan Fante

If your lover is a dog – love dogs
If your heart is in the sea – love the sea
If your feet are on the sands of the desert – love the desert

But nothing is to be gained here on my broken TV set without life's gift of uncertainty
No peace
No enduring love
No self contained paradise
Can or will be mine until I appreciate my own lost-ness

Perhaps then, I am Dante - or Caligula
But who I am really
is not what I considered myself to be
I am a being within a being
a heart beating within a heart
a whisper contained within a scream

I am the tiles on your church floor and the shit on your streets
I am my greatest friend and my most hated enemy
I am a part of history and the hope of the future
I am the man next to you on the train - or your most feared executioner

I am my own best friend in a world of orchestrated chaos
In fact - I am a piece of eternity

I am who I say I am.

Strangely, my experience is that man is most perfect when he
believes himself to be lost

Mercury in Retrograde

By Iris De Anda

Silly Girl
who do you think you are?
always blaming the stars
playing with fire
dancing at the edge
falling into dark corners
there is a guardian
roaming above your head
the reason you're not dead yet
always taunting
split second chances
runaway chases
take another sip
forget remembering
slip into night sky
don't care
play music loud
fast and louder
invoke wonder
thru muses
infuse this mess
you find yourself in
come up for air
come down from there
the ladder is waiting
the moon is lighting
the earth is calling you home

Ode to a Morning Paper

By F. Douglas Brown

we've come up together   hand in
hand   my blood   your ink

you've kept me
honest with the day

state taxes and sports ready
the given grind of events

this world would ruffle us both
could leave it as if it weren't

for my kin   leave it the
way a paper boy tosses you   thump

down   jumpstart my morning
walk back to retirement's ease and pillow

and that's for me   earned time to be
with you   meanwhile your job is one bit

shock and awe   grief and national
mourning   the king of pop is dead at 50

is sharing my morning coffee
goddamn it   I say

but you don't flinch   never
budge   the same resolve mama taught us

you bring me back to her
send me home to cook for my brothers

out of school to work with her
when she was sick   like her you tell me

I'm a man every morning
you flip your white wings and the span

of my face unfolds
I swallow the facts   march if need be

or bet on them horses   wave
a fly away   vote the idea

of a black president to life
and we sho' did, baby   we sho' did

darlin'   I frame your fringe and
frock to my wall   at least the parts

telling me black folks can live
other than how we been living

Jacob Lawrence Ekphrasis: Frederick Douglass Series

By F. Douglas Brown

Panel 7. olemarsterauldsaythisthegospeltruththatifyouteachthatniggertoread
therebenokeepinghim,andthaswhutmakemewoki'swoktowriteantoreadghazal

Ole Mr. Auld said, if you teach that nigger to read
there be no keeping him, so I became determined to read.

I saved biscuits and jam for the poor white boys, traded a piece of pork
for pencils and paper, or a lesson on cursive or a story read

aloud by someone who knew the correct pronunciation.
Sometimes I'd sing a bit, lull them to nap so I could read

an extra passage or poem. I could feel my stars alter their path,
a grand achievement evolving. To write is to fill my belly; To read,

is a pail of coal I can throw onto a fire deep inside me.
My heart burns through page after page. Read-

ing to the sunrise was not wise, but the risk was what I knew.
Like my mother, I only have a small torch to guide me. When I read,

I re-route her hideous twelve miles. By day, I hide books in holes,
brush the dirt off every night. Most of the time, I am alone, read-

ing to myself. Frederick Douglass, how spoiled you are to have a weapon
of this size. Freedom radiates from my face with each word I read.

5th and Spring Street

By Ramón García

The words of Central American and Korean
street preachers
hurled upon the noisy rabble of day crowds.

Words of damnation
beyond individual hysteria
"Repent! Jesus is Coming!"
Prophecies absorbed by the city's brutal ignorant hunger,
they enter the body where sin slumbers.

Rooftop Party

By Ramón García

Ten miles in the night distance
the San Gabriel mountains were burning.

A sublime image of flames climbing
the graded darkness of mountains, flames that in the day
melded into sunlight and bellowing smoke.

Flaring winds blazed the hours, pacing and
Consuming them.

Someone, predictably, commented "Rome..."
And passed the empanadas.
"I drove my car up there," Patssi said,
"I had to see it up close."

Juan Gabriel Ascends to Heaven

By Ramón García

Scaling the lyrics of an orphaned soul
Singing is a ladder, we are the steps,
You will reach heaven.

You remained the same on both sides of the border.
Everything changed, but your songs carried on
Untouched by the vicissitudes of alienation.

Somehow you were always there....in the blank spots
Of time, a constant, irrefutable
Promise, a sad celebration, emotional carnival...

On the radio, all those childhood Sundays before mass,
Lyric indulgences
Foretelling private tragedies.
College years, the apartment with the shag green carpet
On Ocean Avenue in Santa Cruz
Will forever harbor the 15-minute Bellas Artes concert version
Of "Hasta que te conocí."
Your voice, flooding speakers in gay bars in San Francisco,
Los Angeles, Buenos Aires, Tijuana, San Diego,
Mexico City...another generation
Will dance, and another and another,
Until there is no trace of who we were—only then
Will your voice disappear...

You ascend the heights of national glory, Oh pure *largesse*.
Angels, those androgynous sluts, await your arrival.
Clouds big as air balloons are mariachis
Playing instruments of unworldly light.
No one will judge you. God will not judge you.
Catholic Mexico never judged you.
God will restore your exalted Ciudad Juárez,
The Ciudad Juárez that is not a graveyard.
And you will again be the Juan Gabriel of the 1970s,
The cute *cachetón* with the sensual Mexican lips,
And the sad eyes.

We will be who we have always been.
We will sing your songs...
We forgive the bad acting and the forgettable movies,
The sincerity of sentimentality.

It was always about the music,
About love–what we could or could not have,

But felt and lived nonetheless,
In those sublime hells of the heart,
The high notes of torment.

Lovelessness, distorted hearts, passion,
Tainted by your songs
Plunged us into the *cursi*.
But we couldn't stop. No, thank God
We couldn't stop ourselves.
Our Mexican lives, cauldrons of contradictions,
Nights of drunkenness and madness,
Your songs redeemed.

You are carrying 1,500 songs
To place at the feet of the Virgen de Guadalupe, or María Félix.

We will make joy of our suffering, your singing insists.
Mariachis send us off when we die.
In the meantime, devalued coins
Replay you in the jukeboxes of survival.

Casualty

BY ALINA NGUYEN

I am a victim of monocles pressed
against muscles. Voices
are images of war
in my head. It hurts,
and I vaguely
know why these days.
It has been so long,
but hurt doesn't leave
even when it starts to forget.
I am tired from banging
my multiplied head.

Attainable Madness

By Alina Nguyen

I don't even know how to introduce myself
anymore, the Hello
my name is is blank.
Its stickiness never touches
my sweater. Somewhere along the way
I peeled so much so the rings on my fingers
no longer texture my identity.
To you, I am nothing, but your couch is your everything.
It won't leave your side, & you've exhausted all your money.
I'm tired of sitting in this murky rental that I thought was beautiful
because I thought you were. I've stared too long
at this candle: the greasy black grains start
to coat everything around us.

Manuel López - El Sereno landscape The place of the flowers

What the Elephants Carry

By Kim Young

A wooden cart   the break beam and axle even the awkward wheels

the elephants can pull through this wide ravine.

One man, perched atop the elephant's broad forehead,   slides slightly to the right,

          as if he might be a great man   the elephants must carry forward.

          The elephants carry. They move forward.

The white hard hats   the men   the leather straps   the bag   the burlap...

What I can say is that I don't know what to ask God.

What do the elephants carry?

I want to tell you something true about myself.

I see the girth of each leg.   The long trunk.

What I see is a downturned look in the eyes.   The man's leg

dangling there over the forehead.

The elephants aren't ashamed.

Cold maybe—   not as in temperature   but a coldness is what they carry.

A resignation.   I love you, token elephants.

God, I want to know what is being carried forward.

Is it sugar   rice   the men's personal belongings   longing?

Angels

Kim Young

When our two dead mothers
sidle out from heaven
they're wearing pink lipstick
and carrying new handbags.
Maybe they've exfoliated
or finally covered the skin
of their purple thighs.
They don't burn in some shine
we wish they might have warmed
us with at night--
instead of chain-smoking
and ripping open packages
of powdered doughnuts.
You're not my child!
they yell as we hacked at our own hair
and pretended the streetlights
could read our thoughts
pretended the horses would
break through the trellises--
the moms with their eyes
us, the little piggies
while secretly we dreamed
their hospital beds might one day
roll wildly down some dark hill
the insurance cards
the long electrical cords.
What terrible child
wouldn't spend a lifetime there
running alongside?

Crows Become a Symbol for the Happiness I Missed

By Kim Young

                                        --for my son

You want to go back   you decide
years later   not a baby anymore—
you want to unknow, find the pouch you left
before you realized all we will relinquish.
    Does everyone have parents?
    Do coyotes have venom?

The nightmares hum behind the drywall
so we keep close sleeping.
Danger is concrete but spreading.
I don't want to die
you say finally
sobbing. *I want to be a baby again—*

I can't take you back   to the park—
you, the infant in a pouch   all stretched out
the strands of your sister's hair stiff
from always chewing.
But I can rewrite—
I can decode from where I sit at a bench past forty
in the trance of my birthday   something like laughter
& above
the crows' dorsal line
stiff & proper   always circling.

I'll take you back   reinterpret
the puppy suddenly loping behind the line
of kids dragging each further into the horizon.
It was just a month ago I pulled you into the world
from my own dark insides.
We push a candle into a glazed donut—
the shadows   nightfall spreading
shiny black crows carving into dusk
a line through time where years later I stumble
back & call it happiness
all new all stretched out.

Now, at night, the cord of your back
becomes a weapon you set down
when you soften against my belly before sleep.
Now, at night, your mind dislodges threat after threat
 I keep you close—
danger concrete but spreading.

I promise to carry you through
the park of this happiness
before you hear the rumble start.

The older I get
the less stiff
the less proper.
I can only burst onto this scene
in retrospect,   the puppy's white teeth
pulling on a rope we follow
like children who don't worry of future things
these worn out symbols of time.

You are the lining
glazed   the best
of what's inside
my shadows are spreading
worn out, opened—
you're not flying
you're carving lines
into the present
until I stumble into a story
I can't I won't
pin down   even if I try.

The Art of Opening up

TERESA CÓRDOVA

We lay in bed holding each other
in a moon-shaped embrace
and talk about the good times,
ones about coming of age.
Bowl haircuts and the social suicide
of our neon colored nineties wear.
You recall the first time feeling loved–
and I my manufacture,
The chiseling of my being into glass
from head to toe in my gritty home
before being shipped off to
the brutal winds of life.

I want to perfect the art of opening
up, instead I close my eyes as
I experience the nirvana from your
whispers in my ear.
Please touch me...
Every half moaned syllable that
comes from your thin cherry lips more cunning than the next.
The laps of your tongue over my
body now a thick layer and succumb
what I am made of.
The planned soliloquy in my head
immersing itself between the sheets
and for a moment
you vindicate my mind
of fragility.

Whine or Whiskey Solution

Teresa Córdova

Walk out of the house,
old man.
Swallow your melancholy down
to the last drop of your whiskey ginger.

Unknown tomorrows
but you want to forget this moment—
hasta que la muerte 'nos separe.

You come back
through the door
groggy eyed, scent of cigarette
from the bar in el ghetto.
With lipstick on your shirt
Inebriated. Thinking you forgot everyone
but your now ex-wife— well,
you tried.

So you wrap yourself in your bed sheets—
they're black. You've morphed them into a coffin,
turned off the lights.

I can hear you from a distance.
The lonely cries, the whispers,
but they are fading.
Your low voice in tune
With your slow heartbeat—
The walls are really caving in now.

She feels like my ghost

ADRIAN CEPEDA

Blinking under covers
some nights I see her spirit
floating above me, blurring
my memory of photographs
feeling her finest white robe
covering her body, her skin
I can almost touch the ripples
of her excitement, tasting
sweetness of wild berry
flavors, her perfume bouquets
a canvas of goosebumps
but all I picture her is haunting
me, gliding out of our bedroom
our sheets tangled by our sweat
our giggles still clinging all of
our nakedness that rings her catcalls
she once purred for me. Although
she has disappeared floating into
someone else's darkness, her
presence still opens up to me
a gift disrobing in smiles,
surprising, beguiled and her
softest skin she loves flashing
her photographic grin, as I inhale
her fabric softness silhouettes
floating as
her cigarette laughter, still flickers
—craving
her steamy aftertaste,
too smoky to forget.

Sententious

KHADIJA ANDERSON

I've moved 1200 miles
for a red and yellow sunset in the desert

I've ripped off my dress
to pay for my daughters college

I've thrown things and broken them
to work for the homeless

I've almost broken the law
to watch a child being born

I've howled at wildfires and the Santa Anas
god knows how I've howled

if 100, then 150

Chiwan Choi

i make street lights appear on the ceiling
until we can no longer be the same

like the red of a house of bricks from childhood
like the dead rising from the pavement in the rain

*

there is an image in my head
of me lying on my back
on the ground outside the world trade center

it was 1989
and gary had told us to do that and look up
he said the building would look like it was going to fall on me

i remember visualizing it as he spoke
i remember lying there on the ground

but i can't ever remember
what it is that i saw
what it was that took my breath away

*

what color am i, father?

*

he looked up at me from the floor
at the bottom of the stairs
briefly
before rolling away so i couldn't see his face

i stood at the top of the stairs
hesitating
as i tried to hide all of my secrets

he couldn't call to me
and i wouldn't run down to him

because neither of us could admit
the distance between us.

*

he stands over me
as i drown in my sweat

he leans down and puts his hands on my legs
holding my knee
like a fruit

rise, he says,
walk.

and there is silence

broken

by a gasp that comes from

deep within me

what happens now

take me to 100, he says.

so i can get to 150.

Ozzie Juarez - Te quiero

I Clean the Cockroaches

ESTELLA RAMIREZ

There are no fireflies here
It's the light pollution
or something else
Whatever the reason
tonight there are
no magical glimpses of luminescence
followed by the dark insect silhouette in the afterglow
The little guys tired after the exertions of glimmering
are easily caught in your hand
to be revered, to recover, to spring off
each shimmer is an invitation to lovemaking
or a warning of proximate danger
but they are not here
We must turn to the cockroach
hiding behind a cup at 4am
a messenger of mutual dark disgust
How does the cockroach invite its lover
something communicated
with its face too small and too knowing
or its prickly legs as it skitters toward her
Yes, it seeks heat as puppies do
With the right conditioning
it will allow you to wipe down
its buzzy coppery wings
allow you to glue precious stones on them
allow you to put a leash around its tiny neck
and yes, it will curl up on the ridge of your collar bone
a living broach, taking only your warmth
and you could hold it
as you would a baby bird
fall in love

Monster Seeking Monsters

ESTELLA RAMIREZ

As a child I saw the naked tail
and glowing bead eyes of a possum.
Not knowing what it was then,
I felt betrayed by my belief
that the world held no monsters.

Other betrayals followed,
the brain in depression
the body binging and purging,
the journal asking why,
receiving poetry as answer.

One day, I went over the rail,
dirt and chipped yellow paint
under my hands as I hopped over,
went down the concrete steps,
crawled inside the culvert.

Monster seeking monsters.

I sought the romance of fear,
the dark, sharp smells, its creatures.
In the dank drain of the city
I found little.
There was the musky smell
of animals and neglect,
the sound of grimy water
traveling in slow droplets.
I thought there'd be
something more:
danger, comfort.

Now when two pairs
of reflective eyes
meet in the night,
when they each startle,
go in separate directions,
I know neither of us is a monster.
Inside me is possum only.

In the dark, frightening,
and in daylight
just a rodent,
timid and innocent.

a black man's heartbreak

Reynaldo Macias

my heart breaks when
black boys fail
to become
black men.

not failing man
hood
just can't duck
bullets
with hands cuffed
in the back seat of a
squad car
they're not Morpheus
hands up still
shot
face down
skittling away from trouble
leaning in car
windows . . . let the music play
lyrical voices call for
help,
last gasps whisper
Mommy or
why?

pac said, "I'll rest when I'm dead."
there are generations
napping.

my heart breaks when
black men flail,
fail on camera, threats called
granddaddy choked into
submission, smiley stu- stu- stuttering that
"None of the p-police
men was black!"

all I have to do is stay
black and
die.

who knew the former would
cause the latter?

Pablo

REYNALDO MACIAS

brown boy growing
up
too fast

yesterday drawing
Daddy
bookmarks today high
school girls and weight
lifting
tomorrow's urgency to
drive
waits, pressing on him
on me
brown boy growing
up
too fast
I can't breathe

teach my son
to be
polite, sit up straight
to protect
and serve him up,
"Speak clearly,"
ask questions expecting
answers
not nightsticks

epidermis a mask
in America
brown boy growing
up
bookmarks begetting
bullets
cute morphing
menace
puberty shooting him up
hands up don't
shoot him
down

can you see he
reads
Percy Jackson novels?
do I tattoo books on his skin?
will the ink deflect hatred?

ignorant systems paint him
dark
on the cover of TIME
under cover of time
how much time does he have?

questions I ask
when he walks out the
door.

Dark Matter

BILLY BURGOS

Things hardly ever change that much.
Emotion reacts like electricity through
the conduits of our bodies. Sometimes there
is light and energy that shows there is activity
in the brown soil. But from a distance the sphere is
blue/green, there are storms that pass around it,
there is love and hate like whispers among
the darkness. There is sound in space that
is similar to what comes from our lips,
this thing we are trying so hard to fight for or
against is a small thing. We are small things.
So when I choose to turn my head away from
the horrors, or hardly have an ability to shoulder
pain I don't beat myself up. All I can do is
moderate the small space I work in, love within
the distance my body transmutes energy in,
have faith in what moves me in a forward direction.
It is all I can do to simplify the already simple,
try to work through an equation of equality that
only matter to us, these whispers hardly taking
up much space at all among the dark matter.

Solfeggietto

She's playing Solfeggietto without a piano,
fingers moving like a spider on fire across
knees coated in acid washed denim.

And we're on a crowded bus, shouldered up
with the mall-bound girls rockin' the fake louie bags,
tribal tights, tapping out their drama on big-faced
Galaxy S4's while hating on the girl with the jazz hands.

But she don't care, she's seeing notes in her head
with Bud Powell whispering, allegro! allegro! while
she coaxes false keys into song. At 43rd Brother Israel
steps on the bus. He is a mixed cat with ginger-toned dreads

and a face sprinkled with freckles that have lived more
life than most folks. He is Leimert Park shaman, wearing
Africa around his neck and silver wrist cuffs like a black Israelite.
He spots her air piano motion and can understand the

voodoo of Bach that's telling her allegro! allegro!
Speaking with eyes closed, he tells her of a universe that
is infinite and black like her and about a God in all that blackness
who has gifted her with those lively fingers and she

is listening while we move past the dug up lots
of Leimert Park being retooled and readied for gentrification
while Bud Powell is in her head whispering, allegro! allegro!
and Africa is in her ears speaking words coated in Patchouli oil.

And by the time we hit King Blvd even the ghetto girls
have put away their phones with the Hello Kitty cases and
are smiling at yo' girl with the jazz hands and thinking

about how good Bach sounds dipping down Crenshaw.

Angel City Review 41

#DTLA is not #Racist!

TEKA LARK FLEMING

The black guy
is masturbating on Sixth again
These homeless people are getting ridiculous
There is this program up north,
where they nicely ship them away for work programs
It is really nice
I don't know if happy adverbs can make an internment camp sound OK
Molina just cares about the Latinos
Molina hates white people
She doesn't have a bike
She didn't go to the bike meeting
We need more cops
We need more security
Another black guy
masturbating
I have a picture, I got up at at 4 a.m. and I caught him
My dog needs a place to run
Can we make that park private?
We are bringing back Broadway
Those businesses weren't real
You know what we mean
I find your accusation that I am racist offensive
Here we go again with the race card, you people and the race card
My name is James T Butts and I am Black and I am here to let you know Bob isn't racist
That black homeless guy is out of control
No one was even talking about race
Obama is the best president ever
This time it's an Asian guy masturbating on Seventh
Did not know they could be homeless?
I thought that was a black thing
What? I am not being offensive just honest
I went out with an Asian lady once
She was real Americanized and talked too much
I had to break up with her
I am not racist, the Irish were the first slaves
I am not Irish, but I could be
There you go again with the race card
Race is relevant here

your accusations of racism
are why you people are masturbating
all over this place
And I voted for Obama,

I told you that.

Fine Art

TEKA LARK

She tracked a cigarette butt into our art gallery
Then she got on her phone
And started texting

She is a symbol of no class

She wouldn't even pick up her dirt when we informed her of her crime
She said she did not bend over
And she didn't look up from her phone
When she said it

It was outrageous

An art gallery is a sacred place
Which is why it we serve wine
An art gallery is a place for those with –
Money
Penises
Expensive degrees
And their girlfriends

Art galleries
Are not places
For filthy chatty vapid whores
Who overshare on Facebook
And track in butts
From the sidewalk

What's that smell?

By Teka Lark

A new fragrance
For you
>   The thin
>   The white
>   The beautiful
For only $350.00
>   You
>>   Can
>>>   Bathe
>>>>   Yourself
In the fragrance of the modern metropolitan white woman
>   "Urban" women can't
>>   Have it
>>>   They are not thin
>>>   They are not white
>>>   They are not beautiful
>>>   They are not racist
>>>>   Not
>>>>>   Like
>>>>>>   You

"What is that smell?"
"Why it is White Fragility (FRA-GEE-LAY-TEE), it's French —I think?"
White Fragility
>   For those who are white, privileged, and are proud of it
"I have white privilege, sorry...." (But not sorry, not really)
At work
Where you are the director/founder/facilitator/whatever for an organization
that helps the

>>>>>   less privileged
>>>>>   less fortunate
>>>>>   less smart (if they
>>>>>   were smart they
>>>>>   wouldn't need you
>>>>>   there to save them)

And your assistant makes you feel
UNCOOOMMFOORTTABBLLLLE
"I'm from here?!" she says.
And you respond, "Everyone is from somewhere!"
That wasn't very nice.

Open your drawer of privilege
Grab your fragrance
And spray
A little bit on
      To feel confident
            More beautiful
            AND Superior
            Because you
            Are definitely
Born with it.

If you Give a Racist a Cookie

By Teka Lark

If you give a racist a rope, they'll want to stay around and ask you about your Black experience .

Then they'll say,
"I was poor too."

When you let the racist get away with that, they'll ask you about music. They'll ask you to play a song and even though the song you played didn't have the N-word in it, when the song is finished they'll say, "Why do Black people get to say the N-word, but white people can't?" But it won't be a real question and they won't say the N-word, they'll use the REAL word.

The racist will then take a look at you. They'll look up and they'll look down and then try to touch your hair and when you move away.

Then they'll say,
"Why are you being so sensitive?"

Then they might bring up OJ Simpson and black-on-black crime.

And then they will get real comfortable and ask you to tell them a bedtime story about you or one of your relatives being abused by the police.

They will then ask for video proof of the story and since you don't have it immediately they'll say, well there are always two sides to every story.

So then you'll spend twenty minutes looking for the video and when you find it and show them they'll STILL say there are two sides to every story and why was your father resisting?

When they are done they'll want to take a selfie with you, so they can post it on social media and show everyone that they have a Black friend — YOU.

And after they do that they'll remember that you're Black and will proceed to choke you with the rope you gave them, because they are scared for their life.

Don't give a racist a rope, because they most probably will strangle you with it
And then— write a book.

Elmer Guevara - Sunday, Working

Echo of the Heart

BY EMILY FERNANDEZ

Know your pain.

We grasp at such truths;
the clumsy metal claw
in an arcade game.

By the time I self-diagnosed:
stress; a knot so tender
in my back,
it sent shocks through my chest,

I had spent nights
contemplating the world sans me,
the mess I'd leave behind.

It started with the question:

What was I worth?

The article, "Women Don't Act
at First Symptoms of Attack,"

and all that rejection too.

I called my doctor,
the appointments made.
Who could ignore the spondee
"Chest pain?"

So I panted on the treadmill,
braless, wires connected.
She said "Keep looking at the flowers
or you'll faint"
as the Chinese peonies throbbed
with each rushed breath.

I lay half naked
on the crinkling paper
the cold wand pressed under breast
revealing the shadows

flashes of fire -- reds and orange --
violet blue specks on the screen

as the whack-back of my beat,
my sound unmuted, saturated
the room.

Twice they saw deviations in the EKG,
an awkward hill, a flattened valley,
but nothing amounting to death.

Know thyself.
 Know thy pain.

How often we cannot
though we feel its intimacy
burn within.

How often stress
makes voodoo dolls of us.
The brain consumes
the body,

Plays its games –
Perpetrator/victim –

until blindfolded
we are bluffed.

Arthur

BY EMILY FERNANDEZ

His mouth: a nascent cave.

The pyretic promise of your magic
dissolves on tongue.

You, the black quixotic monster,
who barely moves a blade
stiff with age and rust
hiding your sober rage

but he mistakes the wind
that whispers in the waves,

tripping in the purple tangle
of weeds, laughing as he crawls
on his knees.

Heaven is a lure
a perfect web of siren stars
your golden song at cliff's edge,

where he falls
for your madman dreams.

Waste of Shame

FRANK MUNDO

I used Google Maps to locate your house,
the streets where you lived, and the empty lot
near the Dairy Queen where your corpse was found
— disgraced, decomposing, head hung in shame —
by a pair of precocious little kids
who could have been brothers like me and you.

These quests, yes, represent much more than you
and some morbid obsession with your house.
Via satellite, hunting down those kids,
— chance excavators of the vacant lot —
I was hoping to undermine the shame
of what had been lost when what had been found.

I just couldn't square that those kids had found
what detectives identified as you.
And so, to put those lying brats to shame,
— along with each crooked cop in that house —
I'd parse the pixels of that parking lot
and show why you can't rely on cops or kids.

But, the lot was always empty — no kids,
no cars, no cops, no answers to be found.
And the detectives *seemed* to care — a lot!
They tried their best to exonerate you,
despite all the evidence in her house
and her skilled performance of grief née shame.

I swear, that ex-wife of yours has no shame!
And she has no business caring for kids.
Why would you ever go back to her house?
Why didn't you call the minute you found
out the cops were investigating you?
It might've helped. It might've helped a lot!

Instead, you did what you did in that lot.
And, while I feel much more anger than shame,
I accept what you did — and I love you;
no matter what your widow tells your kids,

no matter what proof those detectives found,
and no matter what happened in that house.

 I searched your house on Google Maps a lot
because lost, I found your haste a waste of shame
for those kids, for those cops — for me and you.

NIGHT & THE CITY: LA NOIR

1.

LA Noir is the other side of Sunshine;
Crime Novels, a Century of scandals:
OJ Simpson to Fatty Arbuckle,
Charlie Chaplin to Phil Spector
Black Dahlia to the Hillside Strangler,
the Night Stalker & Charles Manson.
Celebrity mansions in Coldwater Canyon.
Mickey Cohen's Haberdashery,
The Doors Live at the Whisky!
Take a left on Doheny,
Unsolved mysteries like Who shot Biggie?

2.

Robert Downey Jr. & Charlie Sheen
Celebrate hedonism's program
Like Lindsay Lohan.
Ike Turner was an old man
Still doing cocaine.
Some hate the player,
Some hate the game.
Southern California seldom rains.
The Landscape of Broken Dreams,
Everything is not what it seems.

3.

Where have you gone Rita Hayworth?
America's first Cover Girl
Divorced from Orson Welles.
"Who knows what evil
Lurks in the hearts of men? The shadow knows."
Literary alcoholics Like F. Scotch Fitzgerald
Came to Hollywood for the paycheck.
Faulkner, Hemingway & Nathaniel West
drank at Musso & Franks.
Basking in B Movies & Ida Lupino
The Outsider under red-lit rain.

Dashiell Hammett wrote The Maltese Falcon,
James M. Cain began his reign
With The Postman Always Rings Twice.
Lucky Luciano & the Sunset Trocadero
Look at Dolores Del Rio on LA Brea,
Celluloid myth & screen legends
Gloria Swanson & Sunset Blvd
Somebody tell Cecil B. Demille
I'm ready for My Close Up.
William S. Hart to Humphrey Bogart,
Belushi OD'd at the Chateau MArmont.

4.

The Hollywood Ten became defendants
McCarthy frightened the country.
Fear ruled the Cold War,
Radicals became scapegoats.
Who Framed Roger Rabbit?
The City of Industry & Chinatown,
Conspiracy Theories abound,
And Most of them are true.

5.

Marilyn Monroe's ghost haunts
The Hollywood Roosevelt,
where the first Oscars were held.
Now they're in a shopping mall.
Everybody's got something to sell,
Drop the velvet curtains
& roll out the red carpet.
The Hollywood myth
Started with Strawberry Fields.
The dirt road called Prospect Avenue
Grew into Hollywood Blvd.
Technicolor marquees & bright lights,
Tabloids publish catfights,
Fans line up on Premiere Nights,
Kodak got the naming rights,
Hollywood's a lot prettier at night.

6.
Bards born under Bogart
Like Suzanne Lummis, LAureL Ann Bogen & Michael C. Ford
Created the poem noir...

Welcome to Beverly Hills.
EL Rancho Rodeo de Las Aguas,
The Gathering of the Waters.
LA Cienega began swamplands,
Cactus gardens & landscape architects
Rows of Palm trees & Eucalyptus,
Purple flowers on Jacarandas,
Towering gates on Westside mansions.
Bette Davis said, "Take Fountain."

7.
Restrictive Housing Covenants imposed social distance,
The struggle for Existence
Causes people to go for broke.
Hollywood is the City of Hope,
Songs of Innocence become Experience,
Dime detectives, dangerous dames,
Dead bodies & late night games.
LA's criminal underworld dates back to the legend of Zorro.
Offshore Gambling ships owned by Bugsy Siegel.
A blanket of lights, the hills are on fire,
The city of night,
Seduced by desire.
Screams heard from afar,
An empty drink in a quiet bar,
A lonely ride in a busted car
Night in the city is L.A. Noir.

Blue Rose

MARCUS CLAYTON

"They're as common as weeds, but you—well, you're Blue Roses!"
"But blue is wrong for roses..."
-From *The Glass Menagerie*

I.
Bleached red petals plucked
from stem spiraled
            on concrete bench
            mirrored each other
                        in floral fringe.

II.
bush with red daisies hung over
    them like a chandelier
s/he cross-legged in chucks
            a body's width apart
            facing each other like a joust
    her eyes on petals
            torn with her fingers
his eyes on her torn fingers

III.
    Do you want to kiss
    an artist with cat scratches
around her palms?
            She paints a red parasol
            with petals
as you two sit alone
converse about Neil Gaiman,
                        Ginsberg,
maybe even Tennessee Williams.
            Do not inch
forward,
look for crows hung
        from her eyes,
perfect white stain circled
    around her ring finger,
look at flowers—no longer paint,
            but a cataclysm of flares.

IV.
Do you want to kiss a boy?
Stares burn the top of your head
white noise slipping through your teeth
as you nervously sculpt a sun
out of daisies and wait
for the real one to go down.
Maybe it will fall into Earth
erase everything like the wind
does the patterned petals that distract
from seared valves opening
in your chest, erase the diamond
resting in your pocket, erase
the red spilled onto the floor.

V.
Below the bench
          inside a backpack tattooed in stiches,
                    a rose—
          petals blue as blood
          that shoots away from lungs.
Above, dusk skates over clouds like a skipped stone.

VI.
Solar flare dispersed
red petals caked under Chucks
blue rose suffocates

Downtown

By Marcus Clayton

...'Well, well, look who's here!" your father yapping
As if you had lost your mind, who never flew,
And landed in L.A. out of the blue—
-James Merrill

blue lights blanket cold concrete in buzzed fluorescence
warms a dirty blonde lying on sidewalk in leopard print
in thin red tee in 50 degree air and warmed by bulb spatter
we step over her to feed a hungry meter one quarter two
quarters three four then pocket the change for bartenders
for cocktail specials and Las Perlas's best tequila mixes
we do not have to cross the street and live in tents
fabric chewed away by mites and patched with spider webs
bed bug sucked thighs and stale whiskey dancing in the teeth
we are the oppressed voices drowned out by speakers
ankles curdled by forty minute lines and forty heads ahead
bartenders eye-fucking for tips swirling mixers like batons
they have to play "How Soon is Now?" once an hour
every hour we smoke and catch our dead breath in night air
we play "what do you see in the clouds" with our plumes
we hope our second hand is not swallowed by vagabonds
but let's call it charity when one hobbles by our herd
and be thankful our legs still work to order another drink
know cops would not put holes in us even with the sun down

II.
lets lace boots to throats of Baltimore blacks lets sing
"Je Suis Charlie" when our tongues are threatened
our mouths should be wild hummingbird wings
shake like pinball at EightyTwo like a spine in a police
truck pitch black '92 streetlights our hands too small
we did not carry Hitachis blame our parent's fingers
blame the knife against James Franco's pens launch
missiles they will not be from our slingshots our American
Spirits gripped in Vs our Kurt Vile crooned into our ears
our porkpies rounded matching curly cues above
lips fists shaken at Hummers barreling down Main rumble
rivals 8,583 shaken like a spine but we heard bullets
enter twelve hearts we heard the first amendment

torn from our throats worst than baby's holed hoodie
torn from mommas breast worst than 41 bullets
guns we do not own guns we do not need as much
as the knives between our teeth we use to cut
we cannot use nigger for our art we cannot see
Mohammad is this punishment we did not put bombs
in the underground plump black bellies with parasites
but we wonder who shoved a blade through Elliott Smith's heart

III
we have never seen rats skate just off the 10 with eyes
to the moon with hands gripping quarters in skinny Levis
but a pink tail slinks between the knees of a set of palms
ashed with frozen scars swatted away by our shoulders
cold as confusion that separates the we when a dollar
slips from your grip into his one less for Angel City
IPAs one less for parking one less we settle
we drink dirty blonde ales under low lights hum
making sure not to spill a drop for thirsty tramps to tongue
to lick like dog bowls from cracks in the 6th Street exit
you claim to towel off the puddle set down your coat
I cannot ground cannot see past chained doors of Angel City.

The Perez Bros - Elysian Park II

A Poem for the Cunt on My Couch

LUIVETTE RESTO

Like an interloper
you walked into my home
without invitation.

So I must ask:
were my sofas soft enough
or did you feel their springs
when you sat down
crossing your Nair enhanced legs?

Did you struggle choosing
from wine glasses
etched with the names of vineyards
and memories you will never know?

Did the bathroom smell
like the entrance to Bath & Body Works?
Did the dishwasher have enough Cascade
to remove your dollar store lipstick
stains from them?

Was my plasma big enough?
The surround sound AMC quality
as you giggled like a child
watching a Disney movie.

Were the wall decorations—

      my college diploma, first publication,
      paintings of Puerto Rican independentistas
      a caricature from my spring break in London

to your satisfaction?

Quality control is important to me
therefore on a scale of zero to ten

      with zero being your return
      to a Bros. Grimm inspired abyss
      for the uninvited

how likely are you to come back?

Drunk Dial

LUIVETTE RESTO

It's 7:30 pm and my mother calls my side of the world
as the sun disappears into the Pacific Ocean

I look at the clock and pray
it's a death, an illness, knowing it's neither.

She drunk dials
but not like the ones we share and laugh with friends at brunch.

Hers are reminders of my laziness, desagradecida
and deficiencies as a daughter.

She tells me how she will die alone
because I won't be there to take care of her
as I recall holding her hair over a toilet bowl,
changing her bed sheets when she could not make it to the bathroom,
or checking up on her breathing in the middle of the night.

Nowadays, I call my mother on Sundays
before the sun disappears into the Atlantic Ocean
as I pray for neither an emergency or an illness.

Overwhelming

LUIVETTE RESTO

—"Personality affects the way a color is perceived on you. If you look best in strong colors and you have a very strong personality, the combination may be too much in some instances. Other people may find you overwhelming." *Conservative Chic: the 5-step program for dressing with style*

overwhelmingly strong: the perfect name for the Macy's fragrance section
overwhelmingly strong: the surprising amount of heavy things I can carry
overwhelmingly strong: what not to write in the cover letter
overwhelmingly strong: the resolve of mothers and caretakers
overwhelmingly strong: what I learned to survive because Audre Lorde was right
overwhelming: the amount of black outfits in my closet
from LBD's to sweater turtlenecks my children affectionately call my poetry outfit
overwhelming: what teaching was like in 2020
overwhelming: the increasing number of children cradled then buried in Gaza

strong: what my therapist reminds me of every other Saturday
strong: what I am tired of being called every other Saturday
when all I want is to come apart like paper mache in the rain

A Woman's Alchemy

Jesse Bliss

No need to tell a pregnant woman how big she looks or doesn't look for where she is
at in her pregnancy
Or what she should put in her body
Or that she will never sleep again
Or have a life
No need
Because her orbit is being dictated by the cosmos
Her poundage determined by the gods
Her intake
Her outtake
Her purpose
Her music
Her muse
Her pains
Her healing
Are far beyond the opinion you carry
Shaped by a society who hides the truths of what bringing a life to this planet actually
entails
Tides rise in her brain, in her being, that are inexplicable
You can call it phrases like "mommy brain" or "nesting"
But from where I sit and where my eyes gaze
And what my mind wraps upon
None of that is the case
In fact
Ancient symbols communicate
And as I struggle to pick objects up off the ground
Or raise myself out of the bed or a car or a chair
As my eyelashes fall to the ground
And my breathing is labored
As my digits swell
And my head bends over the toilet another time
I know this great creation
Exits
To bloom the blossoms of sacred eternity
Exploding inside me
A spindle
Weaving a magic beyond comprehension
Creation is messy
Creation is messy
Creation is messy

And to be respected
Some of the greatest warriors in history brought life here
So don't clown
Or underestimate what a woman can do with a babe in her arms
The alchemy she can create
Illuminating the healing of century old stuck
Stop buying into the western world's way of putting a woman in her place
Stop and reconsider
Chose something different
This piece is dedicated to the voice in me
That no longer need be silent
And in turn the collective voice
By giving voice
And speaking truth
We instantly being to transmute the ignorance
And recreate the paradigm

Innominate Panorama

WILL ALEXANDER

Being a rush of myth & vapour
there exists a panoramic fog of poetic jackals' blazes
appearing on lower planes as the froth of refraction

here
there exists the scarlet base of bluish jaguar's ink
of sculpted swans within the air of seminal polar initiation
not unlike the dialectics of water
having the somnolent power of vertiginous cobalt emanation

each meadow of ferociousness bleating
like a naked armistice of smoking sanguinary flowers
evolving higher & higher into hackias of crystal
into elliptical meridians
far beyond protoplasmic complication

one then sees a realm of lighted Impeyan pheasants
flying in circles in a violet unicorn's palace
where there electrically proliferates
ozonal spells
osmotic snows
being flakes of weightless rainbow jonquils
transcending the dark
of oily dragon fang auroras

Sun As Indigenous Psychic Flare

WILL ALEXANDER

Sun
in the "Marsians"
in the "Ophiogenes
in the clan of the "Senegambia"
as blood bearer
as Plesiosaur's odour
like a spell encrypted with python dice
invisibly worn like medieval armilausas
so that one's inner cobalt shimmers
taking on a kind of jimson impersonation
coming into view as perfect cultural aurora

perhaps as gorgeous Aztec obsidian
riding a purplish Appaloosa into the turbelarian waves of the
Syrian Orontes
 knowing its seasonal aridity to be of smoking gallstone amber
 to be of telepathic aurality
  not unlike eruptive synaesthesia
or Euphratian cosmic irrigation

 there exists its theophany of exile lavas
 its icy monastery of peril
 its heavenly ice hunt shadows
 its curious downpour obscuration

 from its hexagonal gulfs
 a livid avalanche of particles
 pouring as carnivorous x-ray diamonds
 seen at first glimpse as murky alkaline vectors
 as savage pituitary forces
 that fuels our fabulous power of blood
 igniting through clouds its winds from crystal lava trees
 not unlike upper ang'elic dialogical enunciation
 being aural stellar mysteriums
 coiled via strabismus as Persian butterfly pyrotechnics

 thus the Sun
 with its meteoritic equators
 spewing incandescent solar brooks
 into the risky jubilation of darkness

so that the human soul sups from its forces
from its blank neutrino winds
from its cosmic nympholepsy vents
swirling within the pineal eye
instantaneous photon blizzards

this being the energy of trance
of blazing phantasmal symbology
like the oscillating core of primordial ochre rubies
all the while 'feeding Saturnian quatrains of agricultural tsunamis
wheat spurs having erupted into sonorous endurance
as diurnal sundials in movement
connected to other solar cascades as vitreous nutrients from
Andromeda
these being puzzling utterance rivers
greenish iceberg squirmings
lit up as phosphorous ointments
rising again as communal Indian integument

The solar form as lion power rhythmic
as boiling termite flower
as velvet solitary riddle
where the sky expands
as an oracular canyon beam
as an aural flare crushing anis into rivulets
turning to greenish Macaw stars erupting from the branches

(the other house)

BY ROCÍO CARLOS

1.
that sleep hammer/ how you hold it
and I let you how I let you/so that we have matching wounds

I put my body between my mother and my sister's body /she never missed I didn't
let her miss. Once, younger, stupid, I ducked or ran from her and I was sorry

what names float the ghost name
the girl who won't come when called
except that I have no name to call her
I use smoke as signals the way my mother does with me
(can a house be built can a house be moved   what is there)
there is
there is
(disappearing people)

2.
breaking as waves as glass slippers/what makers demand
what salt is: protection against the works of others
or misfortune
what is language but tripwire/or a bridge
from far away sisters wave to us
the hand that holds your name like longing /when
I put my teeth together to say your first syllable my mouth waters with sorrow

3.
(which flood)

(joy)

stubborn door, this skin
and burial in this body sounds of laughter and breaking and instruments the
body as instrument the line of a childhood a turning away or running away /
wilderness/ starting from a home to a world/ a life the ocean for the first time

(the first time the tide lapped at my ankles I wept with shame/I apologize mother
this is my body/my father held my hand and laughed at the water).

and burial and burial and burial a song again a lingering and forming how like a
life how the body becomes and then disappears
mother who gives permission to cry who makes the rain and drought
mountains crumble so that forests can rise under the feet of wolves
(something about peaches and moons/a potted mint and portraiture)
and what things quake, a limb, a lip, the continent with my desire for your
trembling and my body as this wilderness what trembling and then stillness
old as wolves I want to hold your face my
(sparrow the kind of bird who keeps secrets)

4.
fever when it comes is a house on fire is the unrelenting rain far from the body
that suffers cold I saw you or the mirage of you or was it your shadow or did I
dream you/ I had a little aunt who was only ash and she never answers when I call
(arrow catcher, here come ashes)

5.
Here is a broken body/ there is a bruised wilderness/ the body in a wilderness
making new an autumn a time of sleep and graying

I picked glass from the soil to protect my family
I nursed a sore paw
the calico follows me wherever I go/
she is not afraid of wolves

6.
But there are fires to forget but we can't forget even when we don't remember
(I remember her/ my color, my scowl the lost twin soul) they say the old dragon
drank to forget her. I think it was to remember. A tired and sad dragon, he was
cruel except to me. His laughter made the doves trill away from the palms. He
lifted me onto the red filly. He told me she was mine and I named her Golondrina,
after the birds that never stay.

you carry the place/ the death/ where is a place not crooked not covered in dust
left by a terrible night left by those wonderful nights and the night of loss too and
the nights of laughter

burn/break/live
or not
some cell in your body deciding what to do what comes next
and the atoms of the universe arrange themselves in such a way
to let you pass.
what the ocean is /what names map/ what use is the body
that can be broken/ or taken/that just fades away.

7.
(Paterfamilias)
a shadow
a bone   its marrow
a hand/ a body
under another's hand and care
a tiny death (mine)
I wait for a sun
I want to be
your first place
that place of
snow marked
by your breath
the Mystery Of
all of the leaving naming and the longing
and I want it to be my name my song
and I am not okay and can't say the words
so I sulk from across the plains and trees
in March there is death and longing and the
month of March does not belong to me

8.
the places where you are from are always
on fire this city or that country or this body
(what if I told you this city of yours is my body
I have mapped it in bridges and train tracks)

el nombre de la estación verano
el nombre de quien / de cual canción

and what are anchors? cement? names? gods?

ghosts: yellow the color of everything but the sun even as it dies in a place so far
from where you were
born/ here in the north your body holds blame

the body /of me
which you conjured
and brought forth in some sleep
(it has been such a long night)

Danie Cansino - It's Time to Make the Donuts

My Father's Falling

BY MELISA MALVIN-MIDDLETON

like the bereft in those television ads
but he calls me instead of pressing some button
that reaches the saints of the elderly at 9-1-1.

I'm not hurt. I just need a little help.

I won't be able to lift him.
Yet I imagine when I arrive
he will be seated on the sofa
with *The Times* in hand
and two cups of peppermint tea.

I swing the front door open in a rush,
finding him prone on the floor,
blood on his pants, biting his pain.
"Did you hurt anything?"

I'm fine.

Rolling him off his stomach, I get a pillow under his head.
"How did you fall?"

I didn't fall. My legs gave out.

I am weak.
No time for ten deep breaths, I try one.
"I can't lift you. I'm calling the paramedics."

NO! he screams.

I wrench everything trying to move the man
who used to carry me,

rush me
to the doctor at two a.m.
and make me laugh
so I wouldn't cry
when the nurse
took my blood. My blood.

I call.

Sirens ascend as they near.

Ode 2

By Sesshu Foster

—for Eetalah and Clarissa

2 in the rain sheets of minneapolis, shivering in ecstasy and caffeine.
2 in the garish noon of bakersfield, shivering in joy and terror.
2 in the basin and ranges of nevada, delivering joy or terror.
2 in the national stadium of chile, american agents stalking.
2 in the liquified muskeg of SE alaska, shivering slightly stalking.
2 in the mild whorishness of the city, shivering in joy and exaltation.
2 in the purposive burning of civilizations, lost in flesh of smoke.
2 in the hurtling automotive spaces of USA, wracked with joy or fear.
2 in rising and falling motion of the Pacific, rolling and trembling.
2 in shopping blocks of downtown boulder, talking poetry and stuff.
2 in the long avenues and boulevards of L.A., cleaning properties.
2 in the pink furled sheets of bedroom, trembling as sleep falls.

the apartheid imagination

BY SESSHU FOSTER

it's the perfect spell, the perfect killing tool, the killing machine.

one million african americans are in u.s. prisons, 400,000 latinos.

they said the war on drugs was a war on the poor, because the institutions are inhabited by the apartheid imagination.

i place this line against the apartheid imagination.

the apartheid imagination requires no location, no physical body; because it has laws, records, court buildings, cells, conversations and life.
it has radio programs, all-white movies, jailhouse mythologies, 2-D images.
before the latest killings started, it was there, and when the killers are forgotten, the apartheid imagination goes on thinking, dreaming up new killers.

who remembers the ones who killed emmet till, medgar evers and fred hampton?
who remembers the guy who shot renisha mcbride?
who cares about aryan nation jason 'gunny' bush who executed jonathan bumstead of the aryan nation also of wenatchee wa for being a 'race traitor' and who shot 9 year old brisenia flores in the face in arivaca az?
who remembers the men of the 11th infantry brigade who machine-gunned the women and children in the ditches of my lai? who remembers names of soldiers of the 7th cavalry who received the national medal of honor for slaughtering 300 men, women and children at wounded knee?
who bothers to remember james earl ray?
who remembers the massacre sites of california?

i place this line in front of the images of trayvon martin, of jordan davis.
i place this line at the images of muhammad al-durrah, iman darweesh al hams, wajih ramahi.

i place this line alongside the images of abdulrahman al-awlaki and brisenia flores.
i place this line transparently over the names of jose antonio elena rodriguez, sergio hernandez gueraca, ramses barron torres.

they were shot by the border patrol, walking or running, shot in the back.
they were killed by israeli forces using 3.1 billion dollars in 2013 u.s. military aid.
they were blown apart by a CIA drone firing a $70,000 agm-114 hellfire missile into a cafe.

they were killed by racists operating out of the apartheid imagination.
the apartheid imagination was created by genocide against indians and slavery of africans as a construction designed to kill white conscience and memory.

anyone entering into the apartheid imagination is a white man or an indian or a rebel slave.

it uses a hegemony of all-white images to convince white people any interest they may have is worth more than any life identified as other. it's a strong mechanism for killing people around the world like indonesia, rwanda, palestine or india.

i have stood in the line for black and brown people at traffic court when i was the whitest one there, and the judge, an asian american guy substituting for the regular judge who was on holiday let everyone go without a fine.

i have stood in my mom's kitchen window on a hill in the city terrace and watched the pillars of smoke rising for days over the city of los angeles.

i have stood at the counter in the laundry of the men's county jail downtown in the fumes of dry cleaning chemicals handing out and collecting bags of laundry and seen the faces of the men in line (where one guy always comes along trying to look like a stone killer and says, "pass me some fucking money or i will fuck you up," and maybe he was a stone killer, but i just returned his stare and took the next guy's bag).
i have waited in the plastic chairs and long lines of the DMV and i have seen who is waiting.

i've had lacerations cleaned out, my face x-rayed and patched up in the ER at county general hospital and seen who is waiting.

i have read poems in front of crowds of hundreds in universities from sf state to naropa, from university of minnesota to suny buffalo and i have looked out on those faces and seen who is walking across the campus at hunters college and cal state fullerton, at the state colleges and the private colleges.

i have seen who is in the jail and in the court house line, who is waiting for a job outside home depot and orchard supply.

i've driven streets of towns of the hinterland where white teenagers scream something out of their cars and race away.

fuck the apartheid imagination, that's what i'm saying, death to the apartheid imagination and its english courses and its ideologies taught in the universities and churches, piss on the all white movies pretending to be set in an all-white los angeles, all-white calif., all-white america, piss on the the norton anthology of post modern all white poetry and the norton anthology of all white american hybrid poetry, piss on all the little cliques of literati publishing all-white catalogs (with maybe one or 2 tokens) and touting another white guy as the latest wonderful thing (that thing is old, it's so old now), arnold schwarzenegger and ronald reagan were your fleeting white icons of pre-eminence, they were happy to see half my family two generations dispossessed and sent to live in horse stalls of santa anita racetrack and colorado river internment camps, happy to go along with lives being destroyed, happy to sign some apology letters decades later, put up a few plaques on historical sites out in the desert.

who remembers individuals operating behind the poison alzheimer's of the apartheid imagination?

who shall remember the mushroom cloud of the apartheid imagination when the next killers are shooting, murder a child in the headlines, and the people post and repost all the images, talking laws, discussing footnotes and factoids?

the names are in the ground, the apartheid imagination like a shadow above them. i place this line in front of it saying my whole life has been against it, and the rest of my life will be against it.

i place this line in front of it.

Statues of the Dead Poets

By Sesshu Foster

Of course the statues of the dead poets are made of words.

Words on lips of students at Calarts, Naropa, CSULA, ELAC.

In theater seats at Beyond Baroque, folding chairs at Midnight Special Bookstore, 2 AM tables at Gorky's and Atomic Cafe.

Phrases flapping like gulls, flitting like swallows, swooping like nighthawks.

Statues of the dead poets stand in the weary morning outside Roscoe's Chicken and Waffles, flicker outside weird midnight motels on Sunset, conjure particulate on really unbearable afternoons.

Statues of the dead poets ride up Angel's Flight funicular only when it's broken down, chow down a fish feast at Ports O'Call, look out of windows of the Million Dollar Hotel Rosslyn.

Statues of the dead poets circle the block to pay to park never again, go through metal detectors at the courthouse never again, talk to a cop with one hand on a Glock, never again.

Statues of the dead poets are spots on the sun when you look up, stars occluded by the glare of avenue streetlamps, moonlight on dirt roads of the Verdugo Hills.

Moonlit coyote shadows across the Hollywood Hills.

We'd make statues of the dead poets from silvery opossum fur, curly mockingbird cries, dry rasp of palm fronds.

Statues of the dead poets in grease-soaked dumpsters behind the buildings, smoldering in a grassfire alongside the Golden State Freeway, tossed like a Frogtown shopping cart in the L.A. River.

Statues of the dead poets: words—-ash.

Words: ash.

Words—-ash and leaves.

A life of taxes paid in words, grit and blood on the teeth.

A life of grief paid in poetry, tenderness, sweetness.

A life of trouble paid in promise, piddly demands, others scoffing.

Statues of the dead poets, Wanda Coleman, Lewis MacAdams, Amy Uyematsu, standing at the edge of the world in the dusty weeds of an open field, gazing across the universe from Santa Monica Bay.

Wanda Coleman's words tasseled blue and gold, flashing like heavy earrings, one quiet evening as we chatted outside the Women's Building, she supported the women reading in the gallery by taking donations at the door.

Wanda's grin might show incisors, but her squint kept a steely reserve, an edge to laughter both exhilaration and derision.

Wanda edited the '92 issue of High Performance Magazine, "The Verdict and the Violence," on the riots/rebellion in the spring, and we read at Midnight Special Bookstore, where she introduced me to her son Ian, but I'd already spent hours lost in those stacks, spent too much money there and every other bookstore I wandered into, carried out stacks of lonely books to study for days and years, while somebody else went to Paris and Hawaii, Squaw Valley and MacDowell, hung out in bars with grad students and academics, divas and their entourage.

Statues of the dead poets in the KPFK archives, Pacifica airwaves of 90.7 FM.

Statues of the dead poets in chapbooks and original editions of Black Sparrow Press books.

Statues of the dead poets recall Jerome's 93 year old grin at Brand Bookstore, Moe's bookstore cigar, Ferlinghetti arranging books in the City Lights window.

Statues of the dead poets indifferent to the quotidian like the clerk at Left Bank Books at Pike Place, Seattle, she didn't even look up but just nodded when I returned forty years later and told her I was glad they were still alive.

Statues of the dead poets implacable like the wet empty streets, early morning outside Pike Place Public Market when you could find parking between produce trucks and fish delivery vans and blackberry brambles in empty lots, but now there's expensive condos and ten thousand tourists crowding everywhere.

Statues of the dead poets know.

The delight of bumble bees.

Blackberries bloom in the beginning of summer.

Hundreds packed the Church in Ocean Park to commemorate Wanda for two days so I drove across town to catch that sea breeze, I stood at the back to watch the poets of the city give tribute to their champion, and Lewis MacAdams joined me with a cane, what's going on? Phlebitis? He looked pale, fragile—*is Lewis shaking*?, "How you doing Lewis?" I asked, "Not good," he replied, maybe he said he was recuperating from a stroke, did I hear right? The speaker at the podium loud, Wanda gigantic on screen behind the the stage, the crowd loud—regardless, Lewis came out to pay tribute.

Then Lewis was gone too.

Statues of the dead poets wrapped in cellophane, bought by a kid at a corner market.

Statues of the dead poets telling your fortune for 5 cents when you step on the scale in front of the liquor store.

Statues of the dead poets stolen for their weight in copper from the Parque de Mexico on Valley Blvd.

Statues of the dead poets dispense ice cream bars or soda cans for quarters at the park outside the gym.

Lewis and I sat around the table for years in the Beyond Baroque bookstore, listening to Fred Dewey rail and rant about not having any money, about needing more money, we gotta bring in more money, sometimes Fred would start screaming. Pam Ward, Viggo Mortensen, who else was on the board of trustees, trying to keep the place alive? I complained about Fred screaming and they told me, "That's just Fred," who raised $100K to pay off the decade of debt and put the city's oldest literary venue back in the black. Lewis was always cool, he was writing a book about the word "cool," how it emerged from 1940's jazz hipster jargon to general overuse by suburban teens everywhere. Lewis always dapper in his cool fedora.

Statues of the dead poets selling tickets from the booth in front of the Rialto.

Statues of the dead poets standing all night under the yellow light of a booth in the vastness of a parking lot on Spring Street.

Statues of the dead poets made of colored plastic on dashboards navigating traffic.

Statues of the dead poets would have more to say, recite a scratchy poem from memory, but their batteries ran out.

Statues of the dead poets half-dressed in mismatched doll clothes or dragged around naked by toddlers.

Wanda's statue sighs like the air brakes of a semi coming down the long incline of I-10 between Quartzite and Desert Center. "*Avoid overheating, turn off A/C.*"

Lewis's statue watches the shift change at the hospital, nurses, PAs, techs and orderlies released into the employee lot as the streetlights wink out, when the sky turns light.

Amy Uyematsu's statue glints and gleams like water in substance and thought, in real and imaginary numbers, fractions and irrational numbers, tracing the long black hair of care along X and Y axes.

Amy's statue made of granite and quartz from the San Gabriel Mountains backlit and illuminated like bright cumulus, as brilliant stratocumulus or cumulonimbus in a breeze over Raul and the generations.

Amy's statue admiring surfers catching waves or coming in off the water, nostalgia in black and white for Toshiro Mifune, revisiting Neruda and Machu Picchu. Cedar, cypress and pine. Eucalyptus, pepper, and jacaranda.

Pine, bamboo, plum, camellias.

Wanda's statue a pinch to grow an inch.

Lewis's statue a ringing in my ears.

Amy's statue says, "Remember Bill Oandasan, Henry Morro, Gil Cuadros, Akilah Oliver. Remember the others, remember also Akilah's son Oluchi Nwadi McDonald, you never met him, but remember Wanda's son too."

Words, ash.

Words: ash.

Fresno Postcard

By Sesshu Foster

One day I'll live in Fresno with the poets. I'll live in Fresno like Gary Soto and Juan Felipe.

I'll live on a side street name F or G, or Mono, or Inyo, or Kern.

A little 1920s wooden house that needs new paint and a new roof, clapboard with bad insulation and swamp coolers hanging off the windows (that almost work if it wasn't over 100 degrees), the house dark and quiet inside so you can hear cars pass in the street.

Horns blast or beats fade away, flies circle at the screen door or in the middle of the living room. Mexican music from a couple houses away. Even under the shade of a tree the sunshine on the sidewalk makes your eyeballs ache.

But I'll walk around the heat where I've never walked around before.

Where Arturo said the ELADATL dirigible lines station was, which he described like it was an abandoned Greyhound depot.

I'll get mutton stew for lunch at a Basque restaurant with Mexicanos staffing the kitchen, a pyramid of fat ceramic cups for coffee, stacks of plastic cups if you want ice water get it yourself.

I'll sit at the formica table with Tabasco sauce, salt, pepper, and a tin paper napkin holder by the window. Thinking about Philip Levine, Omar Salinas and William Saroyan. I'll open a book by Joseph Rios, Anthony Cody or Mai Der Vang, read some poems and think about them. Annotate or write in the books if I feel like it.

I might get inspired and have to write something right there.

I'll look out the window and think, here I am in the capital of poets, here I am in Fresno.

Erick Medel - Young Familia

Denning

BY TRISTA PAYTE

Listen.
I know this den holds you
too tight, these familial ties
biting limbs grown longer than mine
despite a canyon of time between.
Years shift beneath skin, reveal the almost-new
slouching toward deliverance and surely
                            this is second coming
        because here you are, this body:
spitting baby teeth, cutting molars
on my exposed and tender wanting.
And I know the snarl in your center aches
to gnash out my smug wisdom—
                because what do those long of tooth know
                about the need to pierce the heart
                of the world?
                        —I know it yearns to feast on this fear-full sincerity,
                let bits collect
in the still pink gum, gather in the down,
leave streaks in the soft fur of your muzzle.

Yet remember. Only a season or two of sleeps
and already you cannot recall who bore whom.
Track these scars we wear together,
marking the day you clawed from marrow,
the day hunger twinned. My not so small;
        body of boy and beastly gaze
        set to loose a hunting upon us all.

But wait.

Because your malnourished mother knows hunger's texture,
how its heat seeps into the cracks of your hands,
makes it difficult to hold
vulnerability
                and resist it.
Your mother knows
you cannot expect such restraint
beyond family embrace.

Your mother knows. Outside this shelter the air springs;
the center holds
mouths and wanting,
rough and round,

        and they are more hungry than you.

Swan Song

by Trista Payte

I glide though these reconstructions—
winter tipped
wings unfurled in offering,
warmth in a moment of singularity.

So why is it
this staggering brood,
this clutch, laid
best of plans aside and stagnant?
Darkling, I never wanted a territorial battle,
a pairing of convenience to forever keep

but now I have lost count of how many ways a body can stretch and twist,
                                        of how many pearls can be swallowed down.
Worrying past hissing breath and two dozen arching vertebrae until
I, Cygnus atratus, belly of bloat and beak of bleating need
         have lost my taste for soft landings,
            stopped believing what hatched could ever hold our fate in the palm of beauty.

But still. I recall
         the lessons of the silk white lake,
         all milk and detachment
         before the cinch of reed encircled breast against shuddered breast.

                        Blessed are those that know the impermanence of creation.

Yet these feathers are soaked
through now,   drunken and staggering,
no grace in the stroke,
                  just lap and nape and webbing mess.

It's true that disenchanted maidens appreciate the trappings
of a good disguise
but you never needed to be held down:

have it your way;
bare and laid in the rushing plunge.

Have it your way, but after this how can body forget the beat—
that strange heart;
this terrible knowledge?

En algún lugar por Tequila o no se donde
Somewhere through Tequila, or I don't know where

By Rosea Cohen-Quezada

En un pueblo de polvo afuera de una ciudad antigua
viajábamos en auto pequeño detrás de camiones y camionetas en carreteras,
rezando oraciones en grupo. Yo iba explorando el paisaje desde un asiento de atrás,
bajo unos audífonos de Walkman.

Éramos cuatro en un carrito carcacha recorriendo calles de polvo
escalando la altitud entre el cielo y el cierro
debajo de árboles de pabellón, bajando burbujas
y dibujando un sol suavecito, tierno, y amarillo.
Estabamos deshaciendo la metrópolis urbana poco a poco
para poner en su lugar lo rural, lo mexicano, lo más allá del programa turístico.

Cambiamos el control remoto y la comodidad de un hotel, por agujeros de culebras
de cascabel y Cocas en botella.
Llegamos a una cuevita escondida en el interior del cerro,
nos quitamos los zapatos y mojámos los pies en una agua burbujeante y caliente
antes de someternos al baño completo en la fuente termal que brotaba de la tierra.

Todos sentados con el agua hasta el ombligo, los adultos pisteando con Estrellitas,
y yo que no me quiero mojar el pelo...
Estoy ahora cazando recuerdos de esa infancia, repasando por el corazón
para volver a estar en ese lugar con todo, por fin dandome ese tímido chapuzón.

Somewhere through Tequila, or I don't know where

By Rosea Cohen-Quezada

In a dusty town outside an old city
We traveled in a small car behind trucks and vans on highways,
saying prayers in a group. I was exploring the landscape from a back seat
under Walkman headphones.

There were four of us in a tiny jalopy traversing dirt roads
climbing the altitude between the sky and the hill
under canopy trees, bringing down bubbles and drawing a soft, tender, yellow sun.
We were deconstructing the urban metropolis bit by bit
to put in its place the rural, the Mexican, that which is beyond the tourist programs.

We exchanged the remote control and the comfort of a hotel for rattlesnake holes
and bottled Cokes. We arrived at a tiny cave hidden in the interior of the hill,
we took off our shoes and soaked our feet in hot, bubbly water
Before bathing completely in the thermal hot springs that sprung up from the earth.

Everyone sat with water up to their navels, the grown-ups drinking Estrellitas,
and I did not want to get my hair wet...
I'm trapping memories from that childhood and passing again through the heart
to be once again in that same place, with everything, finally making that timid splash

Oil and water

By Anahita Safarzadeh

Consumed by petrichor
where it rains despair

insert images of broken trees.

Viscosity overwhelms our skin
with permission from cavities in our minds
getting ourselves lost
to remember what it felt like to be
found.

Then, the seasons change
again   we must change
boxed in "freedoms"
and choices of organic devastation-
      hyper objects passing on treadmills stuck on high speeds
      SLICK
Oil stains skin black full melatonin pores clogged drain.
Infinite choices
      water can't wash away
      It's too bad my pen only works under water

Lost in reveries of washing blood while washing blood
      off walls.
Is shitting where you eat a way of claiming territory?
And all else - what all else?
Lunatics remain
to howl at unripe moon left on vine and hollywood.
Rotten roots-
spoiled fruit can't stop dinner of starving feasts.

Sun beams off ends
crisping lasting flakes,
the last flakes.
These don't belong here.
They don't belong to me.

What's the difference between
A settler and an alien when both immigrate?

She looks up at the night sky - point up.

This one, she says, this one is covered
in stars
ash and that   dark blue.
What gives a foreigner
          It's foreignness

What happens 25 pages into your book
when you only write under water?

Semisupervised learning
a process by which __ points
          and __ writes
          while __ edits.

I've gotten it wrong again-
I'm getting it wrong again.
And now - lost in the silver hum of electromagnetic signals
I'm too far to notice the trees from the trees
-the scientist from the analyst.

This pen is wet
          are my thoughts this easy to paint?

A woman who can manipulate her world
to believe she is a man
Doesn't notice she does it everyday
          Not just while they watch her
          Not just while they watch her
          Not just while they watch her
Buffering
Oh, it this growth?
          pending

Stuffing her pants with a cucumber
while she tapes down her 34 d's
grows out armpit hair but not beard
only cute on skinny white girls with lesbian tendencies.
She goes home to take off her disguise
-at least the parts that she can.

They warned her it would be hard
-the world and the joining in.

They have a pill for that.

Ends up making her tits fall off.
She grows a small penis
and covers it.
Brush strokes
on papyrus.

Nothing is waterproof
until you hear that
the buddhists are killing the muslims
and then you know it-
that the proof is in the resistance.

Wanders outside of the pack once
And calls herself an entrepreneur
-there are too many broken links on the internet to create a real connection.

Not In Defense of Masculinity

By Janice Lobo Sapiago

Not even when Binh was peer pressured into freestyling in Vietnamese or when
Jonah was the only dude of the group of bros who volunteered to ride with me in my
brother's Corolla to In-N-Out or when Omar agreed with me that he liked Danity
Kane and missed girl groups, too or when no one clapped when I bowled a strike but
high-fived me when I hit two or three pins when they didn't know I bowled with my
brother every Sunday for a whole academic quarter so he could practice & especially
not cuz we both listened to Native Guns or Logic or even Common whoever called
themselves conscious & not the time when Joe voluntarily showed me and Ana his
scrotum before we watched Gladys at the choir recital in the school cafeteria, how
it looked like rotten blackberries with the white fuzz fungi you only throw away or
like when I told Eric that Darius gave me the sweetest moment in kindergarten when
he gently pulled my cardigan off my shoulders and placed it in my cubby next to his
but then forgot and claims he never did that & when in seventh grade I sat on the
bench next to Martín who said that I should sit on his lap because I was his girlfriend
like he truly believed all dogs go to heaven or some shit like Gustavo smacking a
girl in the arm in fourth grade because her ponytail smacked him square in the face
like she planned that when that girl was me like how dare I flex the muscle of my jet
black hair to his crown or how could there be a whole world against him you know
there are students in my classroom who still think everything I say is a suggestion &
how someone told them a degree makes you a better person & how often we bury
stories six feet deep inside us without a tombstone so that we don't have to go back
and find what we abandoned so what does 'on purpose' mean again? and can you tell
these bi(nary) boys that it's like when Porsha & Tessa & Gail said we should shave
everything yup all of it like a conveyor belt of self-extraction and bodies built strength
from cat calls and how many times we joked the other was a ho so much that even my
immigrant mom said it to my third gen-American best friend and how he laughed the
courageous belief boys laugh when we refuse their generosity at bars and never when
we don't get recognized as femicide or even bullshit at our sudden deaths by law or
white women's kindness far gone are the days where I won't lunge back breaking glass
coming out of the hiding men whipped with the softest sides of them

vernacular

ma, on your maiden voyage,
seawater soaked
 your travel suit.
for your first meal here, you boiled
your clothes in a pot:
       salt collected and
       cleaved to the circular rim.
ma, how did chicken taste,
       its flavor extracted by oceanic sediments?
your child was an anchor in the kitchen sink,
cry snagged
       by rocks piped in airways.
her first breath made a plunging exchange
exchange of elements

water to air. ma,

show me how to kiss
the top of your
salt and pepper head.
whet me into lyrics worth rescuing
and i will brine your meal in fixed silence
at every port
       lining the bloated sea.

94 Angel City Review

vinegar

in a dream, i am in my high school gymnasium
standing in line for southern ribs.
smoked ribs wafting, glistening red in
north carolina barbeque sauce.

not the bland south carolina recipe.

im talking about a generous vinegary concoction
paprika, pepper, cayenne and dripped
in oh, that smooth
thick
golden
honey.

my mouth waters, vinegar shimmies her malty
taste down my tongue. she pauses at the taste buds, tells
me she has read all the books in the galaxy. in darkness,
she held prismatic knowledge, turned and turned, light
contemplating through.
while she bubbled ethanal and oxygen,
anticipating birth, she thought about settling as beer, a faster
process. but the secret of life, she tells me
is here.

ba ba joins me in line,
hungry for all the books in the galaxy. a
white woman behind us yells,
"this is america.
we wait in line, we wait our turn,
chink." she yells until she is red as bbq sauce, red
drunk from power. but ba ba,

he smiles at her,
southern smile, buddha eyes,
vinegary patience.

when i woke up, my forefinger and thumb were
pinched together by north carolina
vinegary bbq sauce dripped in oh, that smooth
thick
golden
honey.

The Perez Bros - La Pacific II

Some Demands

By Lexi Cary

I'll be ready to make up with Jesus for real
If he gives me west-facing windows for life,
Indoor plants that never die,
And an empty cistern for a heart
That swirls continually with incense smoke,
So as to repel trauma from its centrifugal force,
So as to give trauma nowhere to lie,
No shadows to return to,
No silver to tarnish.

I'll make up with Jesus
If he can prove he can make me slippery,
Evasive, strong-kneed and ready to run,
If he can heal my skin to make me less delicate,
Less rose petals, less satin.
If he can dry my tear ducts for one month,
Make me forget the sound of sobbing
Over what Ariana Grande must be going though,
The fleeting feeling of young love,
How it refreshes like lemon water
But sours just as fast.

Jesus, I told you already I don't have time
To fix my brokenness before approaching you.
I'm starting to believe a narrative of healing
Is misapplied to the heart.
The way I miss you isn't chronological.
I miss the blinding teen devotion,
The certainty in the darkness of my bedroom.
More than I wanted to make out with anyone that moved,
I knew that you not only existed, but loved me.

All I know for sure now is that seasons will pass,
Young love will flare out, and I'll be left sobbing about it
In yoga, lying in savasana, fists closed tight to keep safe,
From a world of uncertainty that scratches your satin skin to shreds
And leaves your fragile heart in the arms of saviors
That want you to crucify yourself with them.

Enough of that.

We Are There

BY CHELSEA BAYOUTH

After they pried Dad's chest open
like a Tomales Bay oyster
to cut the cancer out
doctors gave instructions
to clap on his back with little rubber things.

Every half hour he braces himself
on the kitchen island of his loft,
Mama and I roll his shirt up,
careful of the stiches
and *pack-pack-pack* on his back.

Sounds like an old jalopy, he says,
and Mama laughs. Three years ago,
just before their divorce,
he demanded we stand
in the kitchen where he screamed,
Your mother is a frigid bitch

so loudly, I wet the bed again.
We soup and tuck. Talk
about getting sweatshirts
that zip up the front
so he doesn't have to raise his arms.
Medication at 2 to move the bowel.
A pan of Mama's enchiladas,
packed the hour drive with towels
to keep them hot.

When our family was young we had a nasty calico
who wouldn't be held and vomited vindictively.
Who, if you got too close, would spit a curled claw
into the tender tips of your fingers. Who we

mourned when we found
her fallen fur
like leaves
across the lawn.

Today

SARAH MARQUEZ

Today, mom told me
not to say a word to the doctor
about the hollow in my breast.
Or the scars carved from porcelain,
streaming down my arm.
She said tell him
how normal you are–
a straight-A student,
4.0 GPA. Smile, like the city
is a happy place,
not overrun with homeless
living out of tents
set up under freeways.
You remember yesterday–
the old woman crossing
the street while the cars were coming?
Forget her. She was sick & you aren't.

What about the shopping carts
collecting in the corner of the block?
What do I say about them?

Nothing. Say nothing at all.

*

They are picked up over the weekend,
& our view of the bougainvillea tree is restored.
I focus on the pink egg-shaped flowers
enticing the bees outside the walls.
Soon, the hive will empty & we won't hear
their loud buzzing anymore.
Silence is the key to ending our suffering.

*

But there's more. The gardener & his sons
forget their footprints in the dirt.
Mom complains how they leave their trash–
greasy Styrofoam boxes, milk cartons, two pairs of gloves.
From my bedroom window, I see them,
hiding in the tall grass; & the broken branch

of the lemon tree– still hanging on.
It might survive if the weather stays warm
for another season, if the birds sing to it,
if no one notices & leaves it alone.

Stray cats prowl the neighborhood
at night. Their glowing eyes see everything.
But who would they tell?
They are also just trying to get by.

*

The Bombay cat stalks me every time
I step outside to check the mail.
Mom reminds me he's only interested
in the small opening between the wall
& the front door. The mice run through
when we aren't watching.

*

One day, I ask: didn't someone die here?
She nods *yes.* One of the neighbors–
a man with white papier-mâché skin.
He used to call to the crows, nesting
in the pines. Now, his wife lives alone
in their one-story home. She sits up
at night, thinking how a little bird pecked
the window for two days the week before.

*

We struggle to pay next month's rent.
I suppose we will move this month.
It's too much– two thousand, four hundred.

Mom is at the hospital overnight,
bent over a patient's bed,
listening for a breath that won't come.
She's never needed anyone.

*

I'm seeing the doctor on Monday,

the first day of fall.
All the leaves are shedding their green suits
for orange, yellow, brown, and red ones.
They work hard too.
Changing is never easy.

*

In the morning, mom appears at the edge of my bed–
a shadow sucking in light. She says, *listen to me M.*

When he asks are you allergic to anything, say nothing.
Hide your pill bottles & tissues in your bag.

When he asks what surgeries you've had, say none.
A gallbladder extraction isn't a big deal. I know the staples
sinking into your skin were awful, but they came out.

When he asks are you depressed, say no.
Conceal those dark circles as best you can.

When he asks are you anxious, don't say I don't know.
Keep your hands to yourself and let the panic rest inside.
It's only one hour of your life.

Wildfire

BY SHANA MIRAMBEAU

I used to love to play with fire.
I would sway my fingers over candles and see how long they could withstand the
flame.

My family thought it strange for me to be so enamored with the flicker of a
lighter,
the stroke of a match.

They would say, "we have to watch this one. You know how she is with those
candles in her room."

    You came in wild that Spring
    All over without aim

    On the day that we met
    Your eyes were of deer, big and bright, stunned by my entrance.
    To me, You were familiar- messy.
    You spoke as if you were the scholar on everything the occult and Tarot.

    But, I was not amused

    Instead

    I felt as though I was walking through the murky of ocean.
    it became difficult to create and hold thoughts in your presence.

In southern California, specific bodies of land must be monitored. The desert winds,
also known as the Santa Ana winds, come in during Autumn, our favorite and your
birthday season , and can create "wildfires."

    We stayed up for hours talking about our joys, I read you my poems, you
shared your drawings with me.

    Every morning I awoke with a salutation from you
    It felt rare because I never had interest to carry conversation over text for
long periods of time, especially with guys, but you were persistent.

    I learned a long time ago to have "tough skin."

    Yet, I let down my guard with you.

I was at the point in my life that I just wanted to be soft, no more fighting.

I thought, "perhaps, he isn't going anywhere."
You sent me songs to listen to and shortly I followed suit.

All the hidden parts I never spoke of with others, you heard.

You were surprised by how much you shared with me, that you missed me if a
few days passed without your eyes upon me, and I was overjoyed to have you see
the part of me that men found intimidating.

Unlike the others, you did not fear my ritual: burning candles, incense, the tarot
and holding rocks to get me through.

I used to love your kind.

And it was more than the Long hair or worn jeans on the verge of tare,
it was the purity of being, no matter how rare
The more unique, the better
The closer to my oddness

Boys: The allegory of my pain, yet the Archetype of my worship

I've seen wildfire take over land,
Moving quickly through the brush-
It's Hard to contain

My belly gave me visions
She warned me of your kind.

I could feel a past- life appearing in my present

shadow work.

By Shana Mirambeau

my mind announced you as the wild I had been seeking. And no one, but me, knew
how deep that narrative was buried within.

Wild was the escape everyone experienced with me, I inherited it from my mother. Everyone came to her for her soothe in words, laughter, and herbal remedies.

I've learned we all have aches, me included.

I was awaiting my own turn at away- a chance to escape.

Into a hidden, a wilderness of sorts.
With every spell cast and candle lit, I remained in the place I knew would entice you. Your kind always liked a good story of "who is afraid of the dark?"

What I enjoy about the unpaved path is the freedom; what I despise is the hard
labor of living, the dismissal of my body. There is so much to learn about standing guard against intruders.
It feels as though there is no parameter one won't dare cross.
In the "out here and over there" comes an active othering and there are seldom
who stay.
They are simply tourists seeking an adventure. They will be the ones to boost how they were there.

There is always an expiration date.

I did not listen to my body's exhaustion.
The high of "us" was electrifying.
It was nice to have someone.

My mother came from a country of hurricanes:known to be the more intense storms that nature could produce.
Caribbean hurricanes begin in June, my birthday season , full of yemaya,
mother, nurture of all who enter her ocean, and end in December, the
winter solstice, a time when the veils are thin, lessons are learned, open your

heart and third eye as ancestors call from beyond.

It's the hot and cold extremes that help create the danger in
storms.

My mother didn't fear the earthquakes of California.
I think mostly because she survived multiple storms with my father
His rage could penetrate cities and leave all of us bewildered.

They say that Cuba has a tendency of holding up well against the hurricanes.

My mother left my father when I was a toddler.

I had to learn to fend for myself early.

You come to me because history has shown you that my skin is porous, and
you
can hide your secrets in me.

But I am no mammy nor mommy.

It's not just you,
It's me, too.
I have a history of my own

It seems as though all the women in my family have been rooted in chaos

My paternal grandmother was the daughter of Haiti: the first country to free
itself from slavery.

She married my grandfather, the " man" of the house, the structure of
authority and power-a provider?
His skin, inherited from his blond hair blue eyed mother, was a trophy.

Yet, he became a storm when the bottle touched his fingers and the liquid ran
down his throat.
There are some stories told and many kept secret about the kind of father he
was, but father always has a way of revealing his kin from time to time.

In Haiti they are known to experience the disasters of earthquakes and
hurricanes.
They build their homes out of concrete, if they have the means, which can

withstand the hurricane, yet leaves them vulnerable to the destruction of
earthquakes.

I've been guessing it's more than how you rebuild. Sometimes, you must leave
for
true safety, if you can.

My grandmother's skin was beautiful and black like night.
But many cannot see in the dark and don't come to help unless you're of day
and white.

I am the one scared of my own patterns- this overwhelming history.

My relationship with men has been disatorrious.

In the past, if my body wasn't sliced into pieces,
pressing down into bars,
 my sweet flesh grilling,

Can you hear me Sizzle?

I'm calling out to you, smell me!

Then, what was my worth?

My step-mother said I would learn the hard way.

You are wild and curious with Colonizer skin

Sometimes the history of your tongue shows itself
I have to be careful that you don't strip me of my resources.

I took photos of the remains left by the Santa Ana winds. They stayed a little
longer than expected this year, but still they left.

The roots of the trees were in conversation with the pavement they once lived
 beneath. They laid there, thick and grander than the sleet gray of sidewalk and
towering over middle paths, streets and even natural soil neighbors.

I walked around the steep holes and there were varying lengths of roots , some
tethered, others uprooted, yet many were holding steady.

What we leave; how we let go. What must remain is a mystery to be played out in bridges.

You count all the women you had and tell me that they all have lived along the foothills.

I wonder if that's all it was-a collecting.

But, you do not count me
            I was never your lady.

Somehow you called me your mentor, your council, your support.
            As if I am your personal altar.

I removed that dare of the name you thought you could brand me
I stepped back from this space of sharing.

                    You were not different

You were and still are   his- story
                            No   ease   son

I
am
A
        real
                woman.

Lately, I have become the verb of storm.

I move sometimes "angrily... [yet mainly] forcefully in a specified direction" reclaiming myself.

Erick Medel - Showtime

I Grew Up Going to la Pulga

BY BRIANA MUÑOZ

- After Daniel Garcia Ordaz

I grew up going to la pulga
every Sunday,
where my grandparents sold
planchas y escobas,
cantaritos y vestidos de ballet folclórico,

sewn by fingers
that pushed colorful fabric
across 32- stitch machine.

My grandma's foot
pressed lightly against the pedal,
in intervals.

In Mexico, my grandmother was a nurse.

I grew up going to la pulga
and sitting on buckets flipped over
while tapping my feet to the music
blaring from neighboring vendor booths
that sold bootleg NB ridaz CDs.

I grew up going to la pulga
where one could find a pair of fresh botines
or first communion gifts,
fruta picada, or caged birds for sale.

When us kids wanted spending money,
our parents would send us to la pulga
to help our grandparents.
All the primos were first introduced
to business, in this manner,

or perhaps, survival.

I grew up going to la pulga
observing men cologned
and suited in tejanas,
wearing their ladies on their arm.
Later, they'd dance a quebradita
at the Friday night baile.

My grandma had nicknames
for every regular, here.
El Jotito
Doña Piojos
La Señora de los Raspados

It was at la pulga,
when attending to my grandparent's customers,
where I learned that my Spanish skills
were at a level of someone
considered to be Pocha.

I grew up going to la pulga
where my "domingo",
a term for allowance,
would be spent at the toy vendor booth

once earned, after a long day's hard work.

For Jack

By Tauri

I let my blind cat lead me into the world

His fur,
petroglyphs of ancestral stories
        etched within the spots
               and manchas of his coat

      He hears the juniper trees morph into lions
           the clouds mold into danzantes—
               the sky drums in feathers and ayoyotes

My blind cat breathes
      life back into himself
             after each seizure

He is exhausted with the stars

I study the astronomy of his nervous system

I arrange his altar:

Orange cat shaped sugar skulls
      Purple sage

Fill his water bowls with cempasúchil
      I light copal

Watch the smoke weave into his whiskers,
         prepare for his transition
              into the spirit realm

I crush his kibbles con un molcajete
  feed him through a syringe
carry him outside with his cobijita
let him feel el solecito

tell him,
      los pajaritos are here to serenade you

In his backyard debajo del sol
      I wait for his body to become soil
      For his body to give life to my ama's lemon trees

I wait to inhale the splutter of his ecosystem
        For his organs to regenerate an orchard of bees

My blind cat leads me into the world

Leads me in visions where desert butterflies & Yucca trees
                trine
                    every
                        planet
                            in our astrology

Lead me into your bloodline, Jack
        I want to know the Mexica Gods you were born after

Lead me into your spirals of curiosity
                fueled from the madness of
                        just being you, Jack

Lead me into love

Lead me where soul leaves ego and all we are
            is you, Jack—
                    Light

Shall We Play A Game?

By Anthony Seidman

If you wake up on your left side, your shoes will last the day. Black sedan will not be parked in front of the doughnut shop where you buy coffee. If you wake up on your right...best speak of rivers, fedoras, and dusk. Don't bend over to pick up a penny. No luck there. If you end the day with pennies in your pocket, throw them in the trash. The result: a restful night, no indigestion. If your spouse falls asleep face-up: comet showers, frayed slippers, dislocated shoulder. If you start your day by stepping forward with your right foot and have yet to sneeze, the rain has been delayed. If your zipper snags, well, you will not attend tomorrow's parties. No more champagne for you! Of course, if you toss a quarter and ask: Heads or Tails? You have been indoctrinated into the wisdom of thin paint on dry-wall. You're exuding the skills of man eating pasta with a single chop-stick. Let's save departure for twilight; the lute's string has yet to be plucked. Let's reserve snail, orange, and cognac. If you step outside your front door and no crow, siesta awaits you. You shall be fruitful, despite your aversion to wash-cloths. Despite dandruff.

Kerotakis

By Anthony Seidman

Now the Verb reaches me via conduits and commixtures: fruit of silence breaking flower into scarlet, cartilage and nerve, tamarind, lemon, sulfur, the opened triptych of thighs whose center panel sweats midnight. In this velvet one can't distinguish camembert from cabernet. Is that grease coagulating on the fields, redolent of garlic and mashed cilantro, or the blackest earth, indistinguishable from blood clotting, bull on hilltop, vinegar pouring on the valley? You Oh Verb rise from the tar. Heaven bubbles with stars and comets. I have levitated, float out the window among black roses, towards the hotel named after your toes. I am reading your hair and sniffing your accent of feverish fans and machetes. Rose of panties scrubbed with soap and left in the shower's stall. Rose of haunted mansions torched centuries ago. Rose of expired postage stamps and kite caught in oak branches. Rose of Rosa, whose name rhymes with everything molten and mortgaged, like atoms, train station, molasses, ivory. Bells, clanging?

Penguin #256 Came to the Zoo with what's Left of His Daughter

By Nicelle Davis

They say I'm making myself ill, but I feel I'm keeping my-
self well—well, as one can holding the dead under tongue.

The Keepers are always rooting around my mouth with their
fingers, trying to uproot my daughter, but I swallow her into

my second stomach and resurrect her once the Vet has gone.
Wellness doesn't concern Keepers so much as the appearance

of care. Way to go. You care. Now let me go look at my wall
and think wall, wall, until all is one and the same wall. What's

left of my daughter is a matted mess of features—I managed
to hold only a beak-full of plume. Nets pulling me one way

and the current her another. When I recall her, I see how she
swam towards nadirs, volume taking her soon, and sooner

upon that soon, by her own valediction. As if all of her could
not wait to be rid of me, but this mouthful of fuzz. How much

of me is her? Her mother never came back. It was just us and
a shared hunger. We went to sea too soon because we had to.

It was go or starve. She wasn't ready. I wasn't ready. There is
never enough time to love any one thing well. Let me look at

this wall. Let me swallow what's left and think wall, wall, wall,
until wall.

Penguin #625 Begins to Suffer from Dissociative Disorder Cause by Repeated Self Inflicted Head Traumas:

By Nicelle Davis

You remember something, something like flying
but of course, you never flew, you never could.

You are in a space so full of birds (who're no sort
of sky) it's impossible to move. Every day you go

to the edge where mouths full of knives flash you.
A glass of forward-facing eyes watches you dive.

Full-force you smack your head against bottom—
at bottom there's a spot marked just from you.

Was this for them? Red turned murky; the stain
mistaken for a hole dug by blood. You can feel

yourself escaping. When you rise, all Penguins
take one step back. *Something mad about this*

one, is what they say about you. *Something mad*
about you, is the only thing Penguins say to you.

Once nearly all Penguin is beat out of you, a set
of forward-facing eyes comes flashing knives

that never bite—the lie of it worse than incision.
Picked up from ground, you are something like

your failings. You are flying outside the ice, and
into a small container where you'll stay until

the bleeding gives up. Healed you'll be returned
to try again. Only harder—to break into liquid sky.

You're a main show attraction—you have become
The Penguin who Wants to Fly.

Why I Am Not a Gravedigger

By Amy Raasch

I like to go to the diner, drink coffee,

and listen to Barbara talk shit. Barbara

doesn't work the graveyard shift.

I tell her, church basement flooded

so we held the reception at the house.

I tell her nobody will sit

in my mother's kitchen chair;

the air is too thick with her

unanswered questions. *Say, A:*

Do you think they'd let me see

the room where Tammy died?

When Mom quit the smokes

cold turkey one July,

Tam set her up on the porch

with a laptop, mug of ice,

and a bowl of cold grapes to binge

the Sweet Adeline convention.

I can still hear her singing

I feel a song coming on

in her chestnut bass tones, years

before the oxygen mask. I'm not

the type to sing while I dig.

Earthworms shouldn't get cut in half

over someone already dead.

My shovel won't break

frozen ground.

I drive by the cemetery,

then leave town.

Ashes

By Amy Raasch

When I turn the card over, the armoire opens to a library
of birch tree-sized books. A pinemarten
claws a spine tattooed with my sister's name,
gnaws its pressed flowers. The ocean forgets

the secret the lake told. Upstairs, my sister
lines a last letter with her perfect penmanship.
A lost dog circles Lake Bde Mka Ska
and what is left of her earthly body.

The deck swirls itself to murmuration,
each black bird a new last word
strung behind a plane-shaped cloud.
Their wing-rustle echoes across lakeskin, a voice

I chase but never catch. I stand at the shore

as fall fires burn, tossing cards in one at a time.

Showering with You

By Mylo Lam

is deterritorialization
           none of me belongs

to me   this water which splits
                  me is yours   yours alone

your look: what are **you**
                       looking at   *Mylo?*

i: *i'm watching how the water sections you*
                             always moving, sometimes

making you whole
                nervously & nakedly

you laugh   i must be transmuting something vague? ridiculous?
                                       live wire & daunting

i wish i could tell you how not to be afraid
                             i don't want to be afraid either

at a point   you've weaponized
                      your long hair a warm starless whip

you mouth me with your mouth

tell you i'm running away
                   just to get back somehow

let's let Sam Cooke sing
                from my little speaker by your tealight

i'm cold again standing in the back
                        you note my trembling

thank god for our small bodies
                  easily swapping positions in the tub

you crouch to keep heat
                              you read your water dripping

down my calves
                    tally the sparse hairs slicked to skin

i sit down
                  penis on your porcelain

you sit too & turn around
                                    scoot into me

i splay my palm on your back
                                      water divides under your blades

see palm trees bleed onto you
                                palm the trees

these trees are just me & my people
                                            palming

i feel so human in here
                          tonight   which means outside   our moons

bloom into sunflowers

All the bullies on the playground,

By Elena Karina Byrne

-after John W. Barger

like parodies of the sacred, all looked like their sport. Small, unburdened bodies
that headed toward the tether ball pole, kickball, handball's floating, flat

concrete walls...children, alive with combat sweat where insults wintered
into gossip across the LA religious school's measured play yard. I knew

I'd perish there, inside each desire to belong to a species of desires.
Everything in childhood begins as a brewing storm upside-down, a secret

writhing feet-first, grass-up. Children, pretending they're someone else
in the mirror, learn to say *No*– –So sockless & muddied, I swung my arms & legs,

climbed into the rattling cage of rolling ocean stones & waves, dove head-first over
backyard brick walls, between other family houses, exhaled with the sun to survive.

Featherless, I'd always find a way to hide in a tree's tangle between daylight
& shade before the bullies could break my ribcage...& for the enemies

as friends who formed their hunger circle around the wounded animal of
my uncertain smile: never again. Pre-teens, in pursuit of a power that's driven

by the same kind of fear & rage crammed like a sailboat inside a bottle that
we bring to school from home, re-invent themselves. Because a childhood fable

multiplies the handed-over story you keep telling your gut. Look at the future's
adult war sinkholes, at the retreating light from your neighbor's window. Now,

see every skinned knee scab I'll pull off more than once in private, just in case
I won't remember the accidental harm, certain to become the rest of us.

Yet how much room for memory there is...

By Elena Karina Byrne

–Hart Crane

      Because this
parallel memory is an open room without
      dance music, yet with gyre erotic & whirl
to wake it, or water-side tumble to make its
      image fall through the body like
a gaze-worthy moon's cast from
the deep pocket of the bad past now
      to litter Hollywood Boulevard
with its out asphalt & recycled glass glitter
that will error erratum in the mind's
      eye for live after-rain light
scattered like utterance: You
& the thank you version of us,
full tangle & in our 6-daily return to
full hours lurid & embedded & lost
      with each raised column of
imagined flower pollen drift
from our room-to-room window when we did
      unconscious ourselves in sex – –
newcomer, latecomer, forerunner of the underground
stream fixed on nothing but more earth,
      everything medians is down the skin center of
what makes us grass kingdom again – – take moving
particles that travel these Pacific-rolled
      horizon sheets
when we dare lose our balance inside of each
other, mocking any on-purpose
final consequence
      that is always certain to give itself
away at the beginning of the film.

Schism

By Taleen Kali

Pleasure is bilateral
Like desire in a distance
A longing
A schism

My heart is an ocean
Feeling the world in waveforms
Each quickening, each tide
I cry every time a cup falls over

New moons split open valves
Carving through the ocean floor
Faint constellations flaming through
And I wish I'd known there was life underneath it all

What do you do with fire in water
Do you pick up the cups that slip through
And what do you do with a heart that spills over
Do you cry for the cups that put out the fire

I have studied much water
And I have played much music
A conductor of tears
Crying is my art form

Maybe then if I can cry in enough cities
and on enough monuments
and on enough shorelines
I will know where to go

Crossing split hairs
Longitudinal lines
Hanging like membranes
Through part of the mind that required a divide to survive

A schism
A woman
A human
An ocean

And if I can keep the cups from falling over
And if the first woman was never broken
And if I studied how to shift tectonic plates
Maybe then I could find a way
To cross the lines

Stand in for Love

By Hannah Pachman

I walk through sulfur filled water.
The creosote
spews from hard desert sand.

I want to sprint, jump and land without pain.

I close my eyes
and pretend something softer
can catch me.

Sometimes people don't say I love you.

I grab a handful of stones.
Sand leaks through my fingers,
as heat from earth's interior rises.

Sometimes it's relieving
to have no clothes on
and stand in for danger.

I haven't done anything.

He raises his eyebrows and smiles,
as I place rocks on his shoulder.

It's awkward to stay friends
with someone you love.

The water stays shallow. I look
at him without touching,
trying not to shiver
in a gust of wind.

I want to hold him close and kiss
the whole day. I can't imagine how
to stay warm without going under.

Sitting in a Vase

By Hannah Pachman

Have you had children yet?
Put on your dancing pants.
Kiss a frog.
Sing about burping.

Let the grim reaper lick your veins.
My mom sent me a bundle of roses.
I stare at them, spaced out between
my thumbs. I give them a week.

I stare at the mold and smell
rotting stems, the chronic illness
that has still not been
solved by medicine.

New life at the cut end
emerges as bacteria. It multiplies,
forms air bubbles
in the stem, blocking water.

When the balloon reaches the sky,
the flowers will be taken off
life support and there will be
someone else's day to idolize.

The wrinkles line up on my forehead,
telling me to sleep for five more hours.
I practice saying my new number out loud,
it sounds like my name fading.

In the subtleties

By Lizeth de la Luz

how do we preserve

  an us

en momentos de p r o m e s a

after

 quiet nights

   moonlit our

s h a d o w s

donde empieza?

 En nuestras manos?

as we cross the street moving a little closer to our steps?

 En nuestros ojos mientras nos balanceamos de los

 que podría ser

  on our lips

  as we say hello?

Affectionate patience,

 trace the divine in me

 por la

  madrugada

   and through coffee stains

 quédate hasta

   enero

create

worlds   **here**
repurpose   your   dark   nights

with   me

Dandelion Tuft

BY LIZETH DE LA LUZ

And I learned

the difference

between craving

and needing

and learned

to shape hunger

learned to store taste

under my tongue

to pour over the "not todays"

a gentle kiss – to be

trapped and to readjust –

to be

  a dandelion tuft

The first visit

By Lizeth de la Luz

I have been talking about you in past tense

Remembering stories from my father's memory

And what I can piece together from photographs

From the outskirts of my last trip to Mexico --

2005 in a booster seat to spend my birthday with

family I thought I'd never see again in flesh and

I'd be lying if I said I hadn't planned out everything I'd say

And the apologies for not being able to visit

& to have you come to us

& for me to see my father be a son

& see your smiles I've only known in pictures explode with laughter

I got to see the continuation of frame

And introduce you to your bisnieto

Who I did not know pondered like you

& for you to see a family that grew out of weeds

And poured into sunrises

I planned to say "hola abuelita" and feel your embrace

Before the hello spilled – fragmented – sprinkled with a

pinch of eyes not strong enough to hold memory readjust

& all I wanted to do was be

TRAFFIC JAMMER, 1973

By Douglas Manuel

Nobody really knows how, but everybody really knows
how it all started—the way history's more, not less,
told from the tip-top of the tongue. Meaning it's a lie,
meaning that it's true to you, you, you, but not me,
me, me. Denise isn't crazy. The white boy slapped her
booty. The newspaper has some of the truth, too: it was
a cake-cutter afro pick that Damon hit that white boy
with. Then, fists, more fists, kicks, knives, and blood.
A school closed for a week. Handcuffs, you know
who wore them: Damon and his friends, all of them,
none of the white boys, none of the teachers who cast
their eyes aside as white fists found Black faces,
as baseball bats and balls, as chemistry beakers, flasks
and test tubes became weapons, as locker doors slammed
shut on Black skulls. Outnumbered as usual, behind
enemy lines as usual, stacked in the back of cop cars
as usual—but no silent swinging bodies this time.

TOAST TO THE FOOL, 1983

By Douglas Manuel

They kissed as if the other's mouth
was the cure for a disease they both
carried for so long they forgot they had it.
A disease no doctors could spot, a sickness
that was beyond the eyes of their cousins,
aunties, uncles, their grandmas,
their grandpas, their mamas, their—

they both didn't have no daddies.

They kissed as if the kiss was the last
thing they would do with their lives,
as if the horns of The End were loud
in their ears, the ground was shifting
below them about to take them forever
under. They both could always see the end
of things, the lastness of last always on—

a dead daddy is a long, long, song.

They kissed as if they were free, as if
the color of their skin didn't scar a target
around their bodies, as if the law couldn't
make them crawl, the police with their
guns drawn, their bodies were sacred
and safe instead of scarce and sacrilegious.
They kissed. They kissed. They kissed
as if music saves, as if loves saves,
because it does. Let's hope it does. It does.

It doesn't.

Manuel López - Somewhere Over East LA

About the Editor:

Zachary C Jensen is a writer, journalist, sometimes translator and educator from Los Angeles, CA. He currently teaches English at various colleges across LA. His work has appeared in LA Record, Cultural Daily, Entropy, Pank, Art Memo, Dispatches From The Poetry Wars, Alligator Zine and other places. He is the Managing and founding Editor of Angel City Review and the editor for the Animals Chapbook Series at Business Bear Press

Artists:

Danie Cansino (b. 1986) is an artist and educator living and working in Los Angeles. Danie Cansino's work manifests in bold chiaroscuro oil paintings and vividly rendered ballpoint drawings on loose-leaf paper, mounted to panel. The subject territory of her drawings and paintings originates from herself, her family members and close friends, and the geography of their shared surroundings - their homes, their neighborhoods, their city. The geographies of the work all stand in evidence of long-standing inhabitation by generations of Cansino's people as they grow up, move forward, and pass on. Cansino describes her work as a love letter to her family, city, and culture, and a remembrance of the suffrage of the Chicanx and Latinx people of Los Angeles.

Manuel López's (b.1983, East Los Angeles, CA) drawings and paintings are informed by his immediate surroundings. Each piece is a careful examination of elements found around his environment: books, records, boxes, houseplants, various elements from his home, his neighborhood, and studio. López relies on observation, memories, materiality, touch, and presence to evoke a feeling of familiarity in the compositions. Manuel López grew up in Boyle Heights and East Los Angeles. He attended East Los Angeles College, transferred to The School of the Art Institute of Chicago (SAIC) where he earned his BFA in painting and drawing. He has exhibited in institutions, galleries, and museums internationally and nationwide including Crocker Art Museum, Atkinson Gallery at Santa Barbara City College, Baik Gallery - Seoul, Vincent Price Art Museum, Charlie James Gallery, and Self Help Graphics among others. He lives and works in East Los Angeles and is represented by Charlie James Gallery.

Ozzie Juarez (b. 1991, Compton, CA) is a multidisciplinary artist who uses the realms of painting and sculpture to honor and revitalize ancient and recent cultural artifacts, languages, and histories. Inspired by the techniques, collaborations, ambitions, and ephemeral qualities of unsanctioned public art, Juarez incorporates excerpts of paintings he observes across the LA landscape into his own work. His ongoing interest in the construction of shared experiences and identities can be equally attributed to time spent as a scenic painter specializing in physical simulation at Disneyland. The omnipresence of American cartoon culture—with its roots in racial stereotypes and its exoticization of global cultures—weaves itself effortlessly into Juarez's motifs.

The Perez Bros eat, breath, photograph and paint lowrider car culture like no one else. Growing up in South Gate, California Alejandro and Vicente (Born 1994) were born into a family of motor-heads, so it was only a matter of time before the identical twins took to documenting the Los Angeles Lowrider culture. Both attended Otis College of Art and Design to pursue degrees in Fine Art focusing on painting, which is when they started collaborating as an artistic duo. Their photographs, murals and paintings capture slices of Los Angeles as only locals can.

Erick Medel (b. 1992, Puebla, Mexico) is a Los Angeles based artist that creates intimate portraits of immigrant life using a sewing machine and thread much like one would use a paintbrush and oils. His canvas is deep blue heavyweight denim, which provides a dark ground that sets off the brightly colored threads that are his chosen medium. Medel draws inspiration from the vibrant Boyle Heights neighborhood outside of his studio, capturing street festivals, sidewalk scenes, and quiet moments in works that tenderly celebrate the joys of a thriving immigrant community.

Elmer Guevara (b.1990) was born and raised in Los Angeles, CA. Guevara's upbringing took place in the South Central neighborhood. In the 1980s, his parents fled a war-torn El Salvador finding refuge in the City of Angels. Along with South Central's vibrant energy and the culture his parents brought with them, he became inspired to reflect on his upbringing and the hybridity of cultures along with the struggles his parents experienced with leaving and adapting to city dwelling. He often constructs narratives by sampling family photos from his youth, reframing compositions that form dialogue about identity and concepts of inter-generational trauma. Furthermore, he depicts observations from his own and neighboring immigrant families and surrounding environment. Reflecting on his adolescence and into his teenage years, he met with friends, commuting throughout the city on public transit and becoming obsessed with exploring the city's crevices. This obsession later opened an appreciation for painting and an education in the arts.

Writers:

Dan Fante is the author of eleven books including Chump Change, 86'd, Mooch, a memoir titled Fante: A Family's Legacy of Writing, Drinking, and Surviving, and the detective-mystery novel Point Doom.

Iris De Anda is a Guanaca Tapatia poet, speaker & musician who has been featured with KPFK & KPFA Pacifica Radio, organized with Academy of American Poets, performed at Los Angeles Latino Book Festival, Feria del Libro Tijuana, Mexico. Author of Codeswitch: Fires from Mi Corazon and Roots of Redemption: You have No Right to Remain Silent (Flowersong Press)

F. Douglas Brown is the author of two poetry collections, *ICON* (Writ Large Press, 2018), and *Zero to Three* (University of Georgia, 2014), winner of the 2013 Cave Canem Poetry Prize selected by US Poet Laureate, Tracy K. Smith. He also co-authored with poet Geffrey Davis, *Begotten* (URB Books, 2016), a chapbook of poetry as part of the Floodgate Poetry Series. Brown, an educator for over 25 years, currently teaches African American Poetry and African American Studies at Loyola High School of Los Angeles, where he serves as the Director of the Office of Equity and Inclusion.

Ramón García is the author of two books of poetry *The Chronicles* (Red Hen Press, 2015) and *Other Countries* (What Books Press, 2010), and a monograph on the artist Ricardo Valverde (University of Minnesota Press, 2013). The Chronicles was a finalist for the Latino International Book Award for Best Poetry Book in English in 2016.

Alina Nguyen was born and raised in Los Angeles, CA. She is the proud daughter of Vietnamese immigrants. Her risograph chapbook, *Before There Were More Ghosts*, was published by Tomorrow Today. She is currently pursuing her Ph.D. in Creative Writing at the University of Nebraska-Lincoln.

Kim Young is an award-winning author of two books of poetry: *Night Radio* and *Tigers*. Her writing has appeared or is forthcoming in Alta, The Cincinnati Review, TriQuarterly, Western Humanities Review, Barrelhouse, LA Review of Books, Los Angeles Review, and other magazines and anthologies.

Teresa Córdova is a writer and academic counselor based in Los Angeles CA. She is currently the Senior Admission Counselor - Transfer/Professionals Program at Cal Lutheran University.

Adrian Ernesto Cepeda is the author of *Speaking con su Sombra* published in 2021 (Alegría Publishing), *We Are the Ones Possessed*, & *La Belle Ajar*, both published by CLASH Books, *Between the Spine* (Picture Show Press), *Flashes & Verses...Becoming Attractions* (Unsolicited Press) and the poetry chapbook *So Many Flowers, So Little Time* (Red Mare Press). His 6th book, the bilingual poetry collection, La Lengua Inside Me, was published by FlowerSong Press in 2023

Khadija Anderson — Muslim, Anarchist, and mother (not necessarily in that order)— returned to her hometown of Los Angeles after 18 years exile in Seattle. Khadija's poetry has been published in Angel City Review, Mobius, Switched-on Guttenberg, About Place, and many other online and print journals and anthologies. Her poem "Islam for Americans" was nominated for a Pushcart Prize and her first book of poetry, *History of Butoh* was published in 2012.

Chiwan Choi is a poet, writer and publisher, author of four full length books of poetry—*The Flood* (Tia Chucha Press, 2010), and the Daughter Trilogy: *Abductions* (Writ Large Press, 2012), and *The Yellow House* (CCM, 2017) & *my name is wolf* (2022) – and multiple poetry chapbooks, including Time Out of Space and lo/fidelity lovesongs. He is a partner at Writ Large Press and an editor at Cultural Daily.

Estella Ramirez is a Mexican-American singer songwriter, poet, and teacher from Laredo, TX. After earning her BA at Johns Hopkins University and MFA at Texas State University, Estella found a nurturing community at Beyond Baroque in Venice, CA. She taught Creative Writing for six years at California School of the Arts – San Gabriel Valley, where she was also the faculty advisor for the student-led, award-winning literary magazine Sugar Pine. She is now the Creative Writing instructor at Keystone School in San Antonio and is currently writing, producing, and releasing new music. You may find her work at estellaramirez.com

Reynaldo Antonio Macías and poetry have been in an on-again, off-again relationship for thirty years. When not stepping out with his words, Reynaldo is a husband, father, teacher, and photographer in Los Angeles, CA

Billy Burgos is an Illustrator/Designer/Poet from Los Angeles. His poetry has been featured in Anthologies and Literary Journals and Zines. He has served as workshop facilitator of the Beyond Baroque Wednesday night workshop and hosted the First Sunday Open Reading at Beyond Baroque. His first full length collection of poetry called *Eulogy to an Unknown tree* was released on Writ Large Press.

Teka Lark is a cli-fi writer, visual artist, essayist, and poet. As a 14th generation African American her work is greatly influenced by the struggle of double consciousness. In 2015, inspired by the Anarchist Book Fair, she founded the Blk Grrrl Book Fair. Her writing has appeared in the LA Weekly, LA Times, Anarres Project for Alternative Futures, Ebony, Counterpunch, Truth Dig, Time, KCET, and Zocalo. Her book *Queen of Inglewood* (Word Palace Press, 2017) explores capitalism and place through dramatic monologue and satire.

Emily Fernandez is the author of the poetry chapbook, *Pliny and Other Problems* (Bamboo Dart Press 2023) and *Procession of Martyrs* (Finishing line Press 2018). She is a professor at Pasadena City College where she teaches composition and poetry.

Frank Mundo is a proud product of the Los Angeles public school, from elementary school to UCLA, where he completed the creative writing program. He is best known for his epic LA poem **The Brubury Tales.**

Mike Sonksen is a 3rd-generation Southern Californian. Poet, professor, journalist, historian & tour-guide, his latest book Letters to My City was published by Writ Large Press. He's written for Poets & Writers, KCET, Alta, Wax Poetics, PBS, LA Taco, LA Review of Books, LAist, Boom and the Academy of American Poets. Sonksen is the Coordinator of the First Year Experience Program at Woodbury University.

Marcus Clayton is a multigenre Afrolatino writer from South Gate, CA, with an M.F.A. in Poetry from CSU Long Beach. He is currently pursuing a PhD in Literature and Creative Writing at the University of Southern California, focusing on intersections between Latinx literature, Black literature, Decolonization, and Punk Rock. Through Glass Poetry Press, he has a poetry chapbook, *Nurture the Open Wounds* and the recently released full-length collection *¡PÓNK!* on Nightboat Books.

Luivette Resto was born in Aguas Buenas, Puerto Rico but proudly raised in the Bronx. She is a CantoMundo and Macondo Fellow. Her two books of poetry *Unfinished Portrait* and *Ascension* have been published by Tía Chucha Press. Her third poetry collection *Living on Islands Not Found on Maps* was published by FlowerSong Press. She is the associate editor of Tía Chucha Press, and she sits on the boards for Women Who Submit and Beyond Baroque. She lives in the San Gabriel Valley.

Jesse Bliss is a playwright, director, producer, actress, poetess and veteran arts educator. System impacted herself, Ms. Bliss has been facilitating theatre and writing workshops in prisons over two decades. Her trilogy, written by BIPOC women writers includes *MATRIARCH, LUMINOUS STREETS: A DTLA Theatrical Tour,* and *WOMEN AT WORK.* Most recently, Ms. Bliss wrote and produced the THE JOY RIDE, a mobile show performed out of vintage convertible exploring matters of racial injustice, COVID-19, friendship and artistry. Ms. Bliss is Co-Producer and Co-Host of KPFK 90.7's THINK OUTSIDE THE CAGE.

Will Alexander is a writer, artist, philosopher, and pianist was born in Los Angeles, California in 1948 and has remained a lifetime resident of the city. He earned a BA in English and creative writing from the University of California–Los Angeles in 1972. Alexander's over two dozen books of poetry include *Across the Vapour Gulf* (2017), *Compression & Purity* (2011), *The Sri Lankan Loxodrome* (2009), *Asia & Haiti* (1995), and *The Stratospheric Canticles* (1995). He has taught at many colleges and universities, including the Jack Kerouac School of Disembodied Poetics, the University of California, and Hofstra University, among others.

Rocío Carlos is the author of *Coyolxhauqui, Los Angeles* (Archetype Press, 2012), *A World Below* (Mindmade books, 2014), and co-author of *ex.her.pt* (wirecutter collective, 2016). Her poems have appeared in Chaparral, Angel City Review, The Spiral Orb and Cultural Weekly.

Melisa Malvin-Middleton is a poet, scriptwriter, actress, artist, and musician who was born and raised in Los Angeles and now resides in Gig Harbor, WA. She is the author of the chapbook Hover the Bones. Her plays have been performed by Savage Players and the Santa Cruz Actors' Theatre. Most recently, the Berkano Gallery in Seattle displayed her acrylic painting in her solo show PNW Sublime.

Sesshu Foster is author of many books including *City of the Future* (Kaya Press, 2018) winner of the CLMP Firecracker Award, and *ELADATL: A History of the East Los Angeles Dirigible Air Transport Lines* (City Lights, 2021), a novel co-authored with artist Arturo Ernesto Romo.

Trista Payte is a writer and educator fom Los Angeles. She holds an Ed.D. from CSUN and is now the director of Mt. SAC writing center.

Rosea Cohen-Quezada lives and loves in Los Angeles. She is a writer and a psychotherapist.

Anahita Safarzadeh is a writer and scholar. she is the author of the poetry chapbook Wolf (Business Bear Press) and is completing her law degree at DePaul College of Law in Chicago where she currently lives with her husband and dog.

Janice Lobo Sapigao (she/her) is a Filipina American poet, writer, and independent scholar from the San Francisco Bay Area (unceded Ohlone land). She is a daughter of immigrants who grew up in a house with 12 people. She is the author of the poetry collections *like a solid to a shadow* (Nightboat Books, 2022) and *microchips for millions* (PAWA, Inc., 2016), along with two other chapbooks.

Shuyu Cao is a Chinese American storyteller who grew up in North Carolina. She currently resides in Los Angeles where she works as a film producer. She is dedicated to excavating the layers of the human condition through all art mediums.

Lexi Cary is a bi writer (w/b)itch and musician based in Los Angeles. Her work can be found or is forthcoming in Germinal Mag, DUM DUM Zine, and Always Crashing. She believes all poems are spells, all songs are poems, and worries that she'll never fully understand her birth chart. You can see more of her work at lexicary.com and @_lexicary on twitter and Instagram.

Chelsea Bayouth is a writer and Emmy Award Winning visual artist from Los Angeles California. Her poetry, essays, and short stories have been published in Nimrod, BOAAT, CALYX, Roanoke Review, and many others. Her manuscript was a semi-finalist in the 2020 YesYes Books competition. More info can be found on her IG @ chelseabayouth

Shana Mirambeau is Multi-disciplinary Creative: Writer, Healer, Intuitive Tarot Reader, and Teacher. Her writing lives within layers of multicultural narrative and Spiritual mysticism. She manages a metaphysical shop where she leads workshops exploring multiple healing modalities for empowerment, Somatic practices for embodiment, and Creative Nonfiction writing classes. Currently, Shana is completing a memoir that explores the process of voice, self, spirit, and healing from intergenerational trauma within the intricate frameworks of an Afro-Caribbean immigrant family in America. Shana resides in Southern California.

Briana Muñoz is a poet from Southern California and the author of two books of poetry including *Loose Lips* (Prickly Pear Publishing) and *Everything is Returned to the Soil* (FlowerSong Press). Her work has been published in the anthologies How to Reimagine America, Beat Not Beat, and Somos Xicanas as well as several literary magazines.

Tauri (they/she) is a poet, mycologist, bontanist, and former chief editor of Acid Verse. They are from East Los Angeles and currently live in the Inland Empire.

Anthony Seidman is a poet and translator from Los Angeles. He has recently published the collection That Beast in the Mirror (Black Herald: Paris, London), as well as the translation of Contra Natura (Cardboard House Press), by Peruvian Rodolfo Hinostroza.

Nicelle Davis is a California poet, collaborator, and performance artist. Her poetry collections include *The Language of Fractions* (Moon Tide Press 2023). *The Walled Wife* (Red Hen Press, 2016), *In the Circus of You* (Rose Metal Press, 2015), *Becoming Judas* (Red Hen Press, 2013), *and Circe* (Lowbrow Press, 2011). *Penguin Noir* recently won the Changing Light Novel in Verse Prize from Livingston Press and will be released Summer of 2025.

Amy Raasch is a Los Angeles-based poet, musician, and performer. She holds a BA from the University of Michigan and an MFA from Bennington Writing Seminars (class of 2024). Her writing has appeared in The Los Angeles Times, The American Journal of Poetry, ANMLY, F(r)iction, and a few anthologies. Her poetry manuscript, *Why I Am Not a Gravedigger* is a 2024 Trio Award Finalist. She writes about what haunts us.

Mylo Lam was born in Vietnam and currently lives in Los Angeles where he grew up. He and his family are refugees from Cambodia. Mylo's work has been published or is forthcoming in The Margins, Guesthouse, Beloit Poetry Journal, Nightboat Books, and elsewhere. His multimedia work won Palette Poetry's Brush & Lyre Prize, his poetry won Blood Orange Review's Emerging Writers Contest, and his chapbook *AND NOT/AND YET* was published by Quarterly West.

Elena Karina Byrne is a Pushcart Prize and Best American Poetry recipient, her five poetry collections include *If This Makes You Nervous* (Omnidawn, 2021) and *No Don't (What Books Press*, 2020). Former Regional Director of the Poetry Society of America, final judge for the PEN's Best of the West award, the Kate & Kingsley Tufts Poetry Awards, and the international Laurel Prize, Elena currently teaches for The Poetry School, Poetry Barn, and Pearl Street at the Fine Arts Work Center.

Taleen Kali is an L.A. native artist, musician, and writer. She's the founder of the experimental DUM DUM Zine & Records. Her debut LP "Flower Of Life" is out now everywhere you listen to music. www.taleenkali.com

Hanna Pachman is a poet, whose work has been published by Rattle, Catamaran, Maudlin House,The MacGuffin, Anti-Heroin Chic, and others. She currently hosts and curates a poetry event which has been running since 2018. Hanna was an Assistant Editor for the poetry magazine, Gyroscope Review for two years. She is attending UCR for an MFA in Creative Writing.

Lizeth De La Luz is a poet, writer, editor, and teaching artist from Southern California. She writes about the frustration of language barriers, learned barriers, and the anxieties of living/loving/grieving in a Mexican body in the United States. Her work has been published in Latin@ Literatures, Acentos Review, and Stonecoast Review among other publications. Find her work at lizethdelaluz.com

Douglas Manuel was born in Anderson, Indiana and now resides in Long Beach, California. He received a BA in Creative Writing from Arizona State University, an MFA in poetry from Butler University, and a PhD in English Literature and Creative Writing from the University of Southern California. He is the author of two collections of poetry, *Testify* (2017) and *Trouble Funk* (2023). His poems and essays can be found in numerous literary journals, magazines, and websites, most recently Zyzzyva, Pleiades, and the New Orleans Review. A recipient of the Dana Gioia Poetry Award and a fellowship from the Borchard Foundation Center on Literary Arts, he is an assistant professor of English at Whittier College and teaches at Spalding University's low-res MFA program.

www.ingramcontent.com/pod-product-compliance
Lightning Source LLC
Chambersburg PA
CBHW060140150626
46550CB00015B/2200